What The Devil Meant For Bad...
God Used For My Good

Overcoming the devil's defeat and strongholds after 20 years

Written By:

Nikki Alexander

What The Devil Meant For Bad... God Used For My Good
By Nikki Alexander

Edited by
Lorraine Elzia

Author's Photographs by
De Ira Lacy

Published by
Rich Living Media
www.richlivingmedia.com
Printed in the USA
All Rights Reserved

For bookings or orders visit
www.nikkialex.net
Email: nikkialexauthor@gmail.com

Social Media
www.facebook.com/nikkialex
www.instagram.com/nikkialexfans
www.twitter.com/nikkialexfans

What The Devil Meant For Bad...
God Used For My Good

Overcoming the devil's defeat and strongholds after 20 years

Dedications

To my heavenly Father and Lord and Savior Jesus Christ, for loving me in spite of my many flaws and constant disobedience.

To my beautiful and hilarious children, M.C.B. and L. Thomas.

To the ministry of Bishop T.D. and Serita Jakes, for the making of the movie *Woman Thou Art Loosed.* It ministered to me and broke some twenty-year-old-strongholds from my mind; inspiring the writing of this book. For this, I am eternally grateful.

Last, but certainly not least, to Joyce Meyer for the writing of *Battlefield of the Mind.* May God continue to bless your ministry and all of the many lives you will impact in the process for the glory of His kingdom.

Contents

PART ONE

Comfort Found in His Word

Introduction

If you are one of the millions of people who have suffered from child abuse, molestation, favoritism, neglect, or who – because of circumstances beyond your control – had an unfortunate childhood…get ready to go get your life back; for everything that was stolen from you will be restored.

The word of God says in Isaiah 61:2-3 NKJV, "To proclaim the acceptable year of the Lord[His favor], and the day of vengeance of our God; to comfort all who mourn; to console those who mourn in Zion; to give them beauty for ashes, the oil of joy for mourning, the garment of praise for the spirit of heaviness [pain & grief]; that they may be called trees of righteousness, the planting of the Lord, that He may be glorified."

Isaiah 61:7-8 says, "Instead of shame and dishonor, you will enjoy a double share of honor. You will possess a double portion of prosperity in your land, and everlasting joy will be yours. For I, the Lord, love justice. I hate robbery and wrongdoing. I will faithfully reward my people for their suffering and make an everlasting covenant with them."

The word of God is truth. Therefore, you must choose to believe it for yourself and know in your heart and soul that no matter what you've been through, God has a purpose for your life. In spite of the trials and storms that you've encountered, remember that you were cast down, but not destroyed. In order to have a testimony, you have to have a test. God will always work things out for your good; just trust Him. Everything the devil has meant for bad, God meant for your good. God has not forgotten all of the pain that you've endured, for He was there with you all along.

CHAPTER ONE

Stolen Innocence

I don't really remember much of anything good about my childhood except receiving Jesus Christ as my personal Savior at the age of eleven back in 1991. I was all legs back then; very thin, medium height and a bright complexion. I was usually a very quiet and observant child, but I was also fun loving and goofy amongst those I felt comfortable with. I remember as a very small child observing a lady at a church who had a powerful anointing when she prayed, spoke and even when she sang. I remember saying aloud, "I don't know what she has, but I want whatever it is for myself." There was a kind lady sitting next to me at the time that heard my comment and began to explain the plan of salvation to me. Even though I was young, her words comforted me as she spoke of redemption, deliverance and eternal happiness. Her face lit up as she told me how Jesus loved me so much that He came and was beaten and died on the cross for all of our sins. She spoke of how He was born through a miraculous birth from Mary who was a virgin, but God touched her womb. She explained that Jesus was teaching in the churches and on the streets when He was about my age. He spent his life here on earth praying and healing others. But because a group of unbelievers did not trust that He was sent by God to save the world, they hung Him on a cross, put nails in his hands and feet and a crown of thorns on His head. He died on the cross and was buried and resurrected and now lives in Heaven. She even took the time to explain the fact that one day He will come back for me and allow me to live in Heaven with Him for eternity. I thought it was so amazing and profound that anyone could truly love me that much, or that anyone could love me at all.

It was hard for me to imagine that kind of love. My parents divorced when I was about a year old and they both were dating other people at the time. Daddy lived with anger and bitterness in his heart toward Momma for years and years to come after the divorce. I used to dread calling him on the phone; his whole conversation consisted of talking about when they were married, how much he hated her and her family, and how much better his life would have been if I weren't born and if they had never married. I always felt so unimportant and unloved listening to his regrets about conceiving me. This drew a huge wedge between him and me. He had four children, and my siblings and I have heard rumors of more siblings that we've never met. Unfortunately, the ones we knew of were by four different women. After he and Momma divorced, he was still young and dating several different women whose children he took better care of than those of us that had his blood running through our veins. *Sad, isn't it?*

Karen, my momma, also dated quite a bit when I was a child. She had three children: my oldest sister Kenya, me—Nikki—the middle daughter, and my youngest sister Teresa. We all have different fathers and unfortunately, mine was the only one of the three men who didn't help out much; financially or otherwise. Momma was a young, single parent who loved her three daughters and she took very good care of us financially. We had the best brand-named clothes and shoes and she always kept our hair done. I am grateful for her hard work and the way she struggled to make ends meet; but unfortunately, she and I didn't have the best relationship a mother and daughter could have and neither did me and my father.

At one particular time, Momma was dating a guy named A.B. When Momma and A.B. first started dating, he was really nice to all of us. He would insist on taking me everywhere he went. One day while we were in the car, he told me to climb onto his lap and pretend I was driving with him. I thought that was the most exciting thing ever. He told me not to tell Momma or she probably would not let me ride with him anymore. So, from then on, every time he went somewhere I wanted to go with him just so I would get a chance to pretend I was driving. After a while, A.B. said that I would have to return the favor and do something for him or he would not let me drive anymore.

"What do you want me to do?" I asked.

"I'll tell you when the time is right and it will be our little secret."

I was very young so I believed it was a privilege to get an opportunity to pretend to be driving. I was excited and too naïve to read between the lines and understand what he meant when he said I would have to return the favor. I would spend most weekends at Daddy's or he would drop me off at my Grandmomma Emily's house on Friday evenings and pick me up on Sunday to take me back home to

Momma. I love Grandmomma Emily dearly. She knows more about me as a person than Daddy ever has because the time I should have been spending with him, I spent with her. She always took very good care of me, along with Daddy's three brothers Uncle Randy, Uncle James and Uncle Curtis. One of the weekends that I was spending at Grandmomma Emily's house – I remember it as if it were yesterday –I was five years old and the year was 1985, my Daddy drove me home that Sunday afternoon. On Sundays, Momma was usually with her sisters at my Grandmomma San's house for dinner. However, Daddy knocked on our front door and A.B. answered.

"Who is it?" a voice said on the other side of the door.

"Alvin," Daddy said.

A.B. opened the door, they greeted one another and A.B. walked away. Upon telling Daddy goodbye, I gave him a hug, a kiss and a very concerned look, but he thought I just wasn't ready to go home yet. He hugged me again and said I'll see you next weekend. What my expression truly meant was, *please don't leave me here alone with this man.*

After I watched Daddy drive away, I saw A.B. walking back into Momma's bedroom. I quickly put my overnight bag in my room and ran and hid underneath the kitchen sink. Just as I had figured would happen, moments later A.B. began to call my name. When I didn't answer, he called me as if we were playing a game of hide and seek.

"Nikki, Nikki, come out! You can run, but you can't hide from me," he said in a child-like voice. I could hear him going from one room to another searching for me and talking to himself. "Remember, if you ever tell anyone about our secret, I promise I will kill you, your momma and your sisters."

Terrified and crying while trying so very hard not to be heard, I still would not respond. All of a sudden, everything in the house became very quiet. Even the television that was on when I got home had been turned off or down; either way, I couldn't hear it anymore and I knew I needed to be very still and very quiet. I covered my mouth and tried to calm my breath so he would not find me.

"Well, since I can't find you, I guess I'll leave you here by yourself."

I heard the front door open and close but I continued to sit there scared to move. All I wanted to hear was Momma's voice letting me know she had come home from my other grandmother's house. . As I continued to sit underneath the kitchen sink, I released my legs from the Indian style position I had been sitting in and put my knees up to lay my head in my hands. I was not going to come out until I knew for sure that the coast was clear. I'm not sure if he heard me move, or if he found me because our apartment was so small and there was nowhere else to search for me, but

suddenly, ending the dead silence, I heard the cabinet doors swing open. "I found you, A.B. said sarcastically while laughing with pride. Since you were hiding from me, I guess I am going to have to make things worse for you."

I was literally trembling with fear. I clutched my knees tighter and my eyes widened. I began crying aloud; begging and pleading. I will be good, just please don't make me play our *secret game*. He then snatched me from underneath the kitchen sink and took me to Momma's room kicking and screaming. I was no match for this man; he was acting as if he'd won the fattest calf at the county fair. He laid me down on her bed and began removing my clothes and kissing me all over. I felt extremely sad and helpless. He was blowing in my ears and then I felt the sensation that had become increasingly familiar as he penetrated me with his fingers. He unzipped his pants and jerked his pants down in one swift move as he took his penis out and tried to put it into my mouth. I moved my head side to side to resist and would not open my mouth, so he put his penis in my ear while pressing himself up against my five-year-old body. His body weight was heavy against me and the grunting sound he was making as he rubbed up against me made my stomach turn. The whole time I was crying, shaking and very confused. I felt dirty and ashamed; wondering what I had done wrong to cause him to treat me like he was. I remember wishing my Momma would just come home and save me. A.B. was so into what he was doing that his eyes were rolling in to the back of his head. He would open them ever so often, just long enough to tell me that this was all my fault and that if I ever told anyone about it, he would kill Momma, my sisters and me. The look in his eyes made me believe him, so I didn't move.

After he was finally done, he rolled over off of me and yelled, "Now take your clothes and get out!"

At the age of five years old, my childhood innocence had already been taken away from me. But, God watched over and took care of me even when I didn't know how to take care of myself. For Romans 8:28 says, "And we know that God causes everything to work together for the good of those who love God and are called according to His purpose for them."

I ran out of there so fast that I could feel the air blowing on my face. I went into the bathroom and quickly locked the door. I still have a habit of locking doors ever since this happened to me. I put my clothes back on and just sat there on the bathroom floor near the door crying because I didn't understand what I had done that was bad enough for me to deserve being treated like I was. I remember being in the bathroom for hours. I didn't want to leave the only place I felt safe at the time. Eventually, I cried myself to sleep while lying on the cold bathroom floor on the rug near the sink. I didn't know what he was doing while I was in there and I didn't want to know, as long as he wasn't looking for me. Still to this day, I have a mental image of his bright-colored penis and I can remember the scent of his body and his breath. It was a foul smell from the saliva he had licked and left all over me.

I don't know how much time had gone by, but I was awakened by a knock on the bathroom door. Frightened, I sat up quickly; afraid to answer. It was Momma. "What are you doing in there?" she asked. I am using the restroom. Okay she said and went into her bedroom. I was so happy to hear her voice; but yet, still somewhat scared to come out. I could hear Kenya and Teresa in our room playing. After trying to wash my face and straighten my hair so Momma wouldn't be alarmed, I finally came out to join them. They were happy to see me and I was surely happy to see them too; more than they knew. Momma heard my voice from her room and she yelled for me to come to her. She said, "Hi" and asked me when I had gotten home. I wouldn't go past the threshold of her bedroom door because I saw A.B. lying there next to her as she sat at the edge of the bed.

"My daddy brought me home not too long ago," I lied and quickly returned to my room.

As the months went on, A.B. continued to molest me every time he felt the need. We moved from one apartment to another across town, and of course, he moved right along with us. I can remember lying awake in bed at night afraid to fall asleep out of fear of waking up with him on top of me. I would try my best to remember to call home before I returned on Sundays, just to see where Momma was. When she would leave us home alone with A.B., I'd always make sure I stayed in the room with my sisters. Sometimes he would call me out of the room to come to him as if he needed to talk to me or needed me to do something and he would always shut the door. Each time he did that, I knew what it meant. It was a code between us that meant that it was time for our secret game. Each time he called for me, I would tremble with fear as I obediently went to him; afraid as usual, and with him daring me to scream or cry as he had his way with me. But he was an authority figure and I did as I was told. There were even some instances when Kenya was away visiting at her daddy's house and Teresa was out of town for the summer with her daddy. Whenever Momma wasn't around and A.B. could get me alone, or take me with him, he definitely took full advantage of those opportunities. I quickly developed a severe amount of distrust for adults. *How could I trust any of them when someone my mother trusted was doing the things he was doing to me?* I was rebelling at school and at home so often that my elementary school counselor said that I would never amount to anything and that I would always be a troublemaker.

After about two years, Momma and A.B. finally broke up and she put him out of the apartment. I don't know why they broke up, but he came back beating on the door one day and she would not let him in. We watched from a window as he broke the windows out of Momma's car. I was glad he was finally gone and out of our lives, but also still very afraid to tell Momma what he had been doing to me. I continued to cry myself to sleep for years, wanting so badly to tell someone, anyone, but I just couldn't bring myself to do it. I just didn't have the courage. He had instilled that much fear in my heart and made me believe that I deserved everything he was doing to me and that it was my fault. I was too naïve to realize that I had done nothing to deserve what he'd done. He was just a sick man with a warped mind and a disgusting sexual desire for children. I was his victim; both mentally and physically

After about six years or so had passed, A.B. came to visit the church one Sunday. I didn't know he was there until after morning Worship. Momma asked me if I remembered him.

"Yes," I answered.

"Well, aren't you going to say Hello?"

"No," I said as I walked away.

She became very upset; she did not understand why I was being so disrespectful to him. She called me back over and tried to make me speak to him and I refused. She had never seen me be so defiant toward her and she slapped me out of embarrassment and showing her disrespect. I can remember thinking, *if she only knew why I didn't want to say anything to that man.* I had begun lying to myself after he left; pretending he'd moved away to California in hopes that I would never have to see his face again. It was my way of coping with what had happened, but I couldn't pretend any longer. Momma insisted I be cordial and show respect to a man I knew had violated me.

"Hello," I said, crying and backing up; afraid he was going to touch me. I could feel my skin crawling just being near him. I could feel my heart racing just from the smell of him so close to me. It was terrible that after all those years, the sound of his voice could still make me tremble; but I certainly did not want to talk to him; let alone allow him to hug me. When he reached out to hug me, I stepped back once more and rolled my eyes; making it very clear that I did not want him touching me.

By the time I was fifteen years old, I had been molested and men-tally abused by not only A.B., but by several other male family mem-bers and friends of the family. My innocence had been stolen time and time again. We had moved into a townhouse and I was going into my first year of high school. The boys my age would always try to get me to have sex with them, but I wouldn't because every time I even thought about it, I would get a mental picture of what it was like with all of the other men who had taken advantage of me in the past. But for some reason, Momma thought I was already sexually active and she would accuse me of it often. Her boyfriend Joel, a Mesquite police officer, was visiting one Saturday morning. Momma had already got-ten up early fussing and cussing as usual. It's like she didn't know any other way to communicate with us if she wasn't yelling and cussing us out. When other people were present that gave her more of an excuse to clown us heavily; especially me. So when the phone rang for me, she began one of her normal tantrums. Every time the phone rang for me, she automatically assumed that it had something to do with sex. What she never knew was she was the one who was putting the idea of sex in my head.

She picked the phone up and then hung it up just as quickly on some unsuspecting soul. I just broke down and started crying profusely, asking her if she could come upstairs to my room since she had company in the living room.

"What is it?" she asked.

For the very first time ever in my life I felt comfortable enough to talk to Momma, or maybe I was just so tired of carrying the weight of the last ten years around and needed to finally release it.

"Can you shut the door?" I asked.

"What is it?" When I didn't answer fast enough, she asked again, "What is it?"

I was still crying so hard that I could barely get my words out.

"I'm not having sex with anyone," I struggled to speak out.

"Well, that's no reason to cry," she said. "That's good because sex is nasty," which is what she would always say.

She never learned quite how to talk to me and explain life; or anything else for that matter. I guess she just didn't feel comfortable discussing things. I tried to calm down and began to explain myself to her.

Finally, I just blurted out, "A.B. started molesting me when I was five. He told me that if I ever told you or anyone else about it that he would kill me, you, Kenya and Teresa. So I have been crying myself to sleep for ten years, afraid to tell anyone."

"What!" Momma screamed in disbelief and she began to cry.

"I am not having sex with the boys at my school," I continued, "because I am afraid and every time I even think about it, I think about him."

"It's not your fault," she said as she hugged, me sitting down on my bed. "I am so sorry that you had to go through that."

We talked for a little while longer and she shared some things with me about her own childhood, but I promised her I would never tell anyone. For the first time I felt a real connection to her. It's sad that it took my outburst about sexual abuse for us to connect, but I was glad that we finally had. I felt as if a great weight had been lifted off of my shoulders and was so relieved. This was one of the first civilized, mother-daughter conversations that she and I had ever had.

After I gave her the details of the secret game A.B. had forced me to play for years, Momma responded, "That's why you've been so nonchalant and standoffish growing up."

She had a concerned expression on her face but was confused about why I'd waited so long to tell her. She had no idea that there was much more to be told about the abuse I had endured, but my spirit had endured enough unleashing for that day. It wasn't until many years later that I told Momma about the other people that had molested me. After I revealed to Momma the terrible experience I'd had with A.B.,

I thought she would start showing me some compassion. I thought she would feel a little guilt and give me a break based solely on sympathy for what I had endured at the hands of a man that she shared her bed with. I even thought that maybe she would understand that I was not a bad child after all, just a child that was misunderstood. All I ever wanted was for her to love me back and to actually start sitting down to talk and get to know me as a person. I wanted her to know the real me. The person I was on the inside. I longed for her to teach me the ways of life and to provide the guidance a mother gives to her daughter. I wanted to feel loved and wanted by her. I needed her friendship, compassion, and I dreamed of being able to share secrets with her or discuss the normal teenage drama from school. Of course, this was not the case. Satan used Momma's behavior to try and prove to me that she didn't love me, nor did anyone else. This was just the beginning of the lies he began putting into my mind. What God showed me years later was that she wasn't a bad mother by choice; she was just a very young, mean and naïve mother. Reality is that momma wasn't able to give me something she did not have inside her to give. She wasn't equipped with the parental wisdom that I'd prayed for her to implement.

CHAPTER TWO

Facing My Own Goliath

We moved around Texas a lot when I was a child; from South Dallas to Pleasant Grove to Mesquite and even once to Tyler. Momma had met another new guy, a truck driver named Lionel. He had custody of his three children; two girls and a boy. Their names were Bianca, Deidra and Samuel. Lionel purchased a three-bedroom house in Tyler and we all moved in together. It was a nice, safe and quiet neighborhood. I liked moving in with his children because Kenya and Teresa didn't play with me much. At the time, I was in the fourth grade. Teresa, Lionel's children and I were all enrolled at Rice Elementary and Kenya went to Hubbard Middle School. The first day at my new school, I met a girl named Monique Johnson. She and I hit it off very well. To this day, Monique says she still remembers my Momma wetting her thumb with spit to wash my face and her tucking my shirt into my pants on my first day of school. Monique lived on our street about six houses away, with her momma Katelyn, her momma's boyfriend Ben and his large dog named King. Monique was an only child.

Momma never had a problem with us spending the night away from home with whomever we wanted to, just as long as we were out of her hair for a while. Monique and I spent the night quite often at each other's house. Katelyn was an Apartment Manager, so in the summer she would sometimes take us to work with her. One afternoon, she left us at their house alone and Monique asked me to come into Katelyn and Ben's bedroom. They had a loft extending from their master bedroom where Ben kept all of his videotapes. Monique apparently had done this before; she went straight to his collection and grabbed a video and we ran back down into the den. She turned on the VCR, pressed play and to my surprise...the video had scenes of two and sometimes three or more people having sex at a time. I had never seen anything like it before. I was shocked, yet curious to see what was going to happen next. We had gotten so mesmerized that when Katelyn came home and pulled up into the garage, we barely had enough time to take the tape out of the VCR before she walked through the back door. Monique snatched the tape out of the machine, turned the VCR off and hid the tape underneath the couch just as her mother walked in the room.

"Hey, what's up girls?" Katelyn said, as she walked through the doorway carrying her briefcase.

"Nothing," Monique and I answered nervously.

Of course, being that we were two very curious eight year olds, and we knew that what we were watching was something that we shouldn't be looking at, we started down a long road to a terrible habit. We couldn't get enough of watching Ben's videos. We would sneak his tapes out of the loft every chance we could get.

Watching pornography became a very bad secret indulgence of mine; it stayed with me long into adulthood. I would watch it every time I was at home alone or really late at night when everyone else was asleep, but not for more than fifteen minutes at a time. I didn't know until years later that what I was watching was called pornography, but even as a young child, I knew it was something I enjoyed watching. It not only intrigued me as a curious child, but as an adult it became a way for me to release stress. . . This activity quickly became one of the many strongholds that I struggled with for years. It was another twisted perspective I had developed about sex. On one level, I realized that my behavior was not normal; but on another, I made excuses for continuing to indulge.

There are millions of men and women, both Christian and non-Christian, who struggle with this same stronghold. I learned later in life that this was a mindset and a form of adultery. The sad thing is that once you've watched pornography, it becomes an overwhelming addiction because you can't get the images out of your head for a very long time..

Pornography, strippers, drinking, drug abuse, prostitution, cheating, lying, stealing and many other habits of this sort are all wrong mindsets and strongholds. They are battles of war that the devil has launched as an attack on the minds of millions of people. I didn't realize the variety of strongholds that Satan was setting up in my mind to destroy my life from a very young age.

Looking back at just how crafty he had been, I began to remember different sexual events that had taken place in my life very early on. There was the time I walked in on Momma performing oral sex when I was three in Patman Switch Apartments. I witnessed her masturbating in bed next to me because she thought I was asleep; and I was four at the time. I was molested by A.B. starting at the age of five. I started experimenting with masturbation at age seven and I was addicted to pornography by age nine. It was a steady progression into a sex addiction.

Once I began watching pornography, I gained a better perspective of how to masturbate and reflect on the images that I had seen in the videos I had watched. My addiction was so powerful that I would often sneak and watch Momma's or my uncle's pornographic VHS tapes while visiting Grandmomma Emily's house. For me, it was not so much the actual event of seeing the sex as it was being able to release some of my anxieties and then I was done with it.

I've never sat through an entire pornographic film because my weakness was always in achieving and orgasm through masturbation. The movie just helped me reach that high faster than I ever could on my own. Of course, being in elementary school at the time, I had no business knowing about sex, masturbation or orgasmic relief. Unfortunately, all of the literature of today only speaks about how men are addicted to pornography; it never provides examples of the many women, children and teens in our society that have the same struggle. Whether through denial or ignorance, our society seems to label addiction to porn as something that only affects adult men, and in doing so, it fails to address how this stronghold touches other segments of our community. It's a dirty little secret; and as a society we like to remain silent to its existence. Even though Monique and I watched pornography almost every chance we got, I never went home and tried to expose my sisters or Lionel's kids to it. I was too afraid they would tell Momma what we had been up to and she would not allow me to be friends with Monique anymore.

*****

Lionel was away from home frequently with his work; so all six of the children in the house would be left at home with Momma. I spent as much time at Monique's playing as I could…anything just to be out of the house. Sometimes Monique would spend the night with me; but for the most part, we were at her house. Monique did not like staying over at our house because Momma was so mean and Kenya was bossy. Kenya was a fire spitting dragon of a big sister. She liked things her way or no way; just like Momma. Kenya could not stand me because I would never comply like the other children in the house. My favorite thing to say to her was, "We're only seventeen months apart!" That would really get her panties in a bunch. Instead of doing as she insisted, often I would laugh at her when she barked out orders just so that I could aggravate her. When I did that, she would finally leave me alone, realizing she could not make me do anything I didn't want to do. We were always confrontational until she would finally leave me alone or Momma would whoop us for fighting or arguing.

We ended up only staying in Tyler for a little over a year. I'm not sure what transpired between Momma and Lionel, but we came home from school one day and she had packed up everything we owned, emptying out his whole house. She said we were moving back to Dallas. We would hear her cussing at him on the phone some nights, but I had no idea, at the time, that things had gotten that bad. I think moving to Tyler was the only time throughout my entire childhood when I had a small sense of balance. Even though we were still being slapped, belittled and embarrassed openly by Momma, the household felt a little more family oriented with the other three kids being there with us and the fact that we had a puppy. The move was good in that regard, but I hated leaving Monique and I thought I would never see her again.

I didn't think my life could get any more complicated after the move back to Dallas; that is up until my step Grandpa Victor died. He was married to Grand momma San – Momma's mother – and I loved him dearly. Grandpa Victor was a generous, kind and loving man; and best of all, he was always fair, no matter what. When we moved to Dallas, Momma had the craziest idea of volunteering for us to move in with Grandmomma San instead of one of her five siblings. He was severely asthmatic and had to use a small breathing machine by day and a much larger one by night. I remember when he would take us with him in his big brown LTD with the blue cab door on the front right passenger side. He would also make us mackerel and flap jacks in the mornings and laugh and play with us. He showed us the kind of unconditional love that we didn't get from Momma or anyone else.

He died unexpectedly of chronic asthma and I was very hurt; but I remember Kenya taking it harder than the rest of us. She was the only one home with him when he passed away and he died in her arms.

Kenya had already been living at Grandmomma San's on and off over the years when Momma, Teresa and I moved in. She had also been one of Grand momma San's favorite grandchildren. Of course, I never made that list. She made it very clear to me as a small child that she didn't like me. I had to finally conclude that people do what they want, when they want and for whom they want. I was one of the favorite grandchildren of my Grandmomma Emily's and I didn't like it that way either. It just didn't seem right to me; I felt like with both of them being grandparents, they shouldn't show more love and favoritism to certain grandchildren and not the others. I felt that way even on the receiving end of the favoritism.

Grandmomma San was a mean, old, shrewd and unfair woman to certain people. But she knew how to be polite at church on Sundays in front of Pastor Garrison. I never quite understood that as a child; it was like she was a transformer or something. She treated me as if she cursed the day I was born throughout my entire childhood and Grandpa Victor was the only one in the family bold enough to stand up to her when she displayed her favoritism between me and the other grandchildren. She was incapable of communicating with me without anger and hatred in her voice. You see, to my understanding, she told Momma after she had Kenya at the age of sixteen, that she would not help her with anymore of her children. Well, Momma not only got pregnant and had me at the age of eighteen, but she married my Daddy against her mother's wishes. This just made the situation worse, because as I've already explained to you, their marriage didn't work out too well at all in the end.

The fact that Grandmomma San wasn't too fond of Daddy didn't help my situation. He would never be disrespectful toward her, but he wasn't too fond of her either; so this put me in the middle of their ongoing beef. As a child, I should not have had to defend myself between the dislikes of two adults. The part I never quite understood though was the fact that Momma had Teresa when she was twenty-one, and yet Teresa made Grandmomma San's favorites list, even though she was born after Kenya and me; and so did a number of some of my other cousins. I never understood why some of Grandmomma San's grandchildren were loved in her eyes, while others made it on her hit list.

I practically begged Momma not to move us in with Grandmomma San, because Momma was aware of her continuously mistreating me. I guess she felt like there was nothing she could do about it with that being her mother and all; but I was still her child. She should have sided with me; the one she gave life to.

God was the only one left to defend me once my Grandpa Victor died. I was so miserable living under the same roof with Grandmomma San; it was unreal. I always felt unwelcome just visiting, but to have to live there day in and day out was quite an unforgettable experience. She smoked cigarettes which I hated. We would wake up every morning to the smell of nicotine and huge clouds of smoke looming over our heads. When Momma worked at night or went clubbing, she would always leave us with Grandmomma San and I felt like an open target. I couldn't breathe wrong without Grandmomma San jumping down my throat. She would literally look for me to do something wrong or provoke me so that she could call Momma at work or tell her when she came home that I had misbehaved or disrespected her in some way. She would try her best to get Momma to whip me when she got home. This happened every night or whenever Momma wasn't around and sometimes right there in her face. Eventually, I started trying to avoid contact with her, the same way I'd taught myself to do with A.B. Of course, just like any other trouble she would always find me. She always looked for an opportunity to have a confrontation with me. I don't think she could sleep very well without commenting on what she thought of my Daddy and me before she went to bed. It was as if belittling me nightly was some sort of sleep aid for her.

We continued to live with her for a while and I hated every moment of it. Grand momma San was so mean and surly that if you were not on her list of favorite grandchildren, you weren't getting jack when Christmas or your birthday rolled around. The one time I remember mentioning my birthday to her was January 14, 1996. For whatever insane reason, I was excited and thought that she would care that it was my birthday, so I went into her room and told her it was my sixteenth birthday. Her exact response was, "I don't know what you're telling me for; I am not giving you anything." As usual, she wiped the smile right off my face. It wasn't that I was actually expecting anything from her anyway; but given the fact that it was a special birthday—my sweet sixteen, I was hoping for her to possibly be kind to me for just once in my life.

I finally just asked flat out, "What did I ever do to you to make you dislike me?"

Her eyes bucked out so big over her glasses, I thought she was gonna fall right out of that old rocking chair she sat in daily. She came up with some lame excuses and was very rude, harsh and surprised that I had the courage to ask her the question that I did. She looked at me in amazement to my boldness and as if she wondered how I knew she didn't like me. Wow! *Go figure.*

Two days later after our discussion, we had another unnecessary conflict; but this time it hit the fan. I was trying to avoid contact with her as usual, and she came into the room where my sisters and I slept. She began complaining, yelling, screaming, ranting and raving about the posters I had hung up on her walls from my *Word Up Magazines* when we first moved in with her. Only this time, I didn't respond in my usual defensive, outspoken manner. I didn't say a word. I just began taking them down off of the walls.

Kenya and her boyfriend Anthony were in our room talking and watching television at the time. When I took the posters down without saying anything in response to her tirade, it still wasn't good enough for Grandmomma San. Her whole intension in coming into the room was to provoke me. So, needless to say, she came back a second time and offered Anthony a Coke, which she kept hidden selfishly with other food and drinks in her closet so no one else could have any.

"No, thank you Mrs. San," said Anthony.

So, I asked, "Can I have one?"

"No!" she yelled. "You just want everything; don't you?"

"No, that's okay," I sighed and put my head down.

"No...you asked for it and now you'd better take it!" she yelled.

"That's okay, it's not even worth all of that," I said as I kept taking my posters down from her walls.

I already knew where she was headed and I was not trying to go down that road with her! Of course, she called Momma on her job exaggerating what happened and making it seem like I had really disrespected her and gotten out of line. I think Momma felt torn between the two of us because as I mentioned previously, she knew Grandmomma San was mistreating me long before we moved in with her, but she had to take her mother's side; right? Too bad it was all at my expense.

The very next morning when Momma got home from work, I had just finished getting dressed for school. Momma was so angry that she grabbed a coax cable from behind the television and she beat me and knocked me down on the floor; kicking me in the side as I laid there in a fetal position. She punched and slapped me until her heart was content; or until her asthma started kicking in, one or the two. I'm sure this was the highlight of Grandmomma San's miserable little life! I still have some of the scars from those frequent beatings from Momma. She used to beat me until my skin would break open and bleed. If I had to describe them, I would say it was like when you boil a hot link and it begins to just split and burst open. By the time she was done, my clothes were ripped apart; I had a blood clot in my left eye and a bloody, swollen bottom lip.

Momma was dating a guy named Randall at the time and he came to pick me up for school. She must have felt guilty, because as we were pulling out of the driveway, she kept repeating threats and yelling out from the front door, "You'd better not run away from home. Be at your

Grandmomma Emily's house no later than ten minutes after 4:00 p.m., or I'll beat you down again!"

Randall is the only man Momma ever dated that all three of her daughters actually liked and trusted; especially me. He has always been calm, soft spoken, understanding and easy to talk to. I was crying so profusely when I got into his car that I could barely catch my breath to stop and explain what happened. He tried to console me and he even explained that he had a grandfather that treated him unfairly as a child too.

When I arrived at school, I still could not stop crying. I tried fanning myself and taking deep breaths, but I just could not stop or control the tears. My hair and clothes were a mess and I had blood on my torn shirt and pants. I didn't want my other classmates to see me that way. I could not see out of my left eye, so it was kind of hard to not think about what had just happened. This was not the first time she had beaten me so badly over nothing; but I guess I just couldn't compose myself. My home girls began to crowd around me asking what was wrong. I had confided in them before about how Momma and Grandmomma San took turns bullying me and most of them had often witnessed it themselves. My good friend Kendall Whiteside was the only one of us who had a car in high school and she tried to offer me some assistance.

"Is there somewhere I can take you?" she asked.

"Yes," I said while sulking and sniffing, "to my boyfriend Benny's house in Mesquite."

My Grandmomma Emily lived right around the corner from the

school but I knew I could not go there because even though she would be very upset to see me all bloody and blistered again, she would definitely call Momma. I knew Benny would be home because he skipped school on a regular basis. So I gave Kendall the directions to his house.

My intensions were to only stay until school was out and Kendall agreed to come back to pick me up before school ended. When we arrived at Benny's house, I walked up to the front door and I knocked very softly. Being the gangster that he was, he became very heated immediately after seeing the bruises on my face.

"Come on in baby," he said. "Are you going to be alright?"

"No," I answered. "I am tired of my Momma and Grandmomma San. It's like Hell on earth living there and knowing all along that she does not want me there and Momma is too afraid of her to take up for me."

Benny and I talked for a long time. He put peroxide and rubbing alcohol on the bruises on my back, arms and legs. Eventually I fell asleep from all of the crying. I was exhausted and had a terrible headache. Matters got much worse later that afternoon when Benny woke me up to get the phone, it was Kendall calling.

"Hello," I said in a low tone, clearing my throat from napping.

"It's three o'clock," said Kendall. "And I am sorry, but there is something wrong with my car. I am not going to be able to come back to pick you up."

"What!" I yelled into the phone. "How in the world am I going to get to Grandmomma Emily's by 4:10 p.m.?"

"I don't know because my dad is on his way to get me and to take a look at my car. I guess I'll see you tomorrow," she said and she hung up the phone.

Every day after school I would normally walk to Grandmomma Emily's house and wait for Momma to pick me up or Daddy would come to take me home. I knew I didn't have anyone else that I could call to get me from way out in Mesquite back to, South Dallas, on time; not without going up for round two with Momma.

By the time 4:15 p.m. rolled around, I was sick at the thought of having to explain to Momma how and why I'd skipped school. "I guess I am an official runaway," I said. Running away was unintentional, but I was so fearful of what would happen if Momma found out. I couldn't simply explain the truth to her and she accept that I was very upset and too ashamed to stay at school. I could not call my own mother for a ride home.

Benny, being the native Californian thug that he was, said "That's alright; you can just stay here with me and my little brother. You don't need them and my mom is hardly ever home anyway."

"That's sweet!" I said. I knew he was angry, but I was smart enough to know I could never live there with him. However, I let him continue to vent.

So the next afternoon when his mom came home, he told her that I attended Mesquite High and lived down the street with my uncle and he didn't get off of work until late so I was coming to their house every afternoon after school until my uncle got off of work. To my amazement and disbelief, his mother bought that lie and sacked it herself.

"Okay that's fine," she said as she walked into her bedroom. Benny and his little brother were practically raising themselves. She was always off somewhere with her boyfriend. She actually reminded me of the constant absence of my own mother, but without the abuse.

On the evening of the next day, the phone rang and Benny and I saw Arsanla Traylor on his caller ID box. It was a call coming from Grandmomma San's house. At first we were afraid to answer it, but out of curiosity, Benny grabbed the phone on the third ring.

"Hello," he said.

"Hi, is this Benny?" the voice on the other end asked.

"Yeah, who's this?"

"This is Randall," the deep voice replied. "Do you know where Nikki is or have you talked to her?"

"No!" Benny said lying. "I haven't talked to her."

"Do you know where she is? She didn't come home from school yesterday and we were just wondering if you knew anything about it? Her momma is worried sick, so if you talk to her please tell her to call home."

"Okay," said Benny and he hung up the phone.

I was listening in on their conversation and I felt bad because I've always loved Randall as if he were my real father. If there was some way he could have come to pick me up and not have taken me home, I would have told him where I was in a heartbeat; but I knew he couldn't have done that.

The next day, Benny's homeboys came by and said that the Mesquite Police were at their school asking around about him and me. I was so afraid after that; I made him turn off all of the lights and the television and we sat there in the dark whispering for hours. While sitting in his room, we saw some flashlights going across the windows in the front and on the side of the house. I panicked and we ran out of the backdoor, across the alley and about two streets over to some bushes on the side of someone else's house. I hid in those bushes for hours in mid-January in freezing weather. Benny covered my white tennis shoes in dirt, brought me a large black bomber jacket and wrapped a blanket around my shivering body. I was there for so long I had fallen asleep and he kept coming back often to check on me. Finally, he came back to get me really late; to come back inside.

On the next evening, Benny had an interview at Pizza Hut and I went along with him. After his mom dropped us off, she went back home. Someone called asking her about me and she told them that she had just dropped us off at the Pizza Hut down the street. While I was sitting there waiting for Benny to come back out of his interview, Momma's ex-boyfriend Joel—the Mesquite Police officer, her oldest sister Sharon—my aunt from hell and the spawn of Satan herself, and my two older cousins: Kelvin and Trina came to pick me up. When they walked through the door, I was sitting there on a bench near the exit. I guess they thought I was going to run, but I just looked up at them. Sharon started yelling and saying how worried Momma had been. All the while I was thinking, *yeah right...she and Grandmomma San were probably relieved that I was gone.*

I got in the car without saying a word the entire time and they took me back to Grandmomma San's house. I just knew Momma was going to beat me senseless as she always had. I was so afraid to get out of the car, but I didn't let it show. When I walked through the door, Momma just stood there crying and looking at me with disappointment in her eyes while her mother and all of her sisters were yelling and screaming at me. I knew she probably was worried about me; but I don't think she ever truly loved me or understood how I felt about living there with her mother.

Kenya finally spoke up in the midst of all of the screaming and chaos and said, "Don't be mad, Nikki told you she didn't want to live here."

No one responded to her. They paused for a split second and went right back to fussing. I still felt great that Kenya tried to protect me and showed me that she cared. Unfortunately, this incident and the time she fought a girl at school for bad mouthing me in her presence, were the first and last time I felt like my big sister was supportive and had my back.

I don't think anyone knows that I really didn't plan to run away from home, it just sort of happened. I was very depressed the entire time I was away. I simply could not fathom why it was so hard for what was supposed to be my own flesh and blood to love and accept me as a person. I know I am not perfect; nor was I the most obedient child in the world by far, but what my family never realized was that my personality of rebellion and bitterness developed from a number of horrible experiences throughout my childhood.

The first of the worst was, having to live with all of the secrets from the age of five without telling a soul for ten whole years. Number two was, not understanding what was so bad about me that I could not possibly be accepted by my own parents, my maternal grandmother or my aunts for no apparent reason.

These things caused me to be a defensive, hard shelled, outspoken, nonchalant and cold individual on the outside; but no one around me ever tried to get to know —the person I truly was. It also made it very hard for me to trust people. I became a product of my own negative environment, and therefore, I reacted in a way that made people think I was a bad person. The only thing I really needed all along was their love and guidance. There's a huge difference in being raised and just growing up. My own family did not know I could sing until they heard it through the grapevine from a friend of the family who heard me singing a solo at a funeral when I was nineteen years old. That's just how out of touch they were with the real me. But even in the midst of being misunderstood, I knew beyond a shadow of any doubt that Randall loved me. He and Momma had gotten so close that he proposed and she accepted. I was beyond thrilled! As the weeks and months rolled by, I marked X's on a calendar daily until we finally moved out of Grandmomma San's house which I commonly referred to my friends as Hell. My very close friend, Quita Washington, still finds this hilarious!

CHAPTER THREE

Hallelujah! I am free! NOT!

Eventually, Momma and Randall got married and we moved into a nice three-bedroom home off of Lake June and Masters in Pleasant Grove. It wasn't that far from Grandmomma San's house, but praise the Lord, it wasn't under the same roof with her either. This was one of the happiest days of my life. I was finally going to be able to feel safe from daily ridicule. I couldn't hide the smile on my face as I packed and taped boxes. I was even singing as I carried them all the way to the moving truck. Grandmomma San just glared at me with hatred in her eyes.

I worked a lot during high school; as a matter of fact, I had been working since I was fourteen years old. I paid for most of my own clothes, shoes, hair, nails, school trips, and senior fees. This wasn't good enough for Momma either. She would always complain about me having my own money and keeping my nails and hair done as if she was jealous. Most parents would have been happy for the help; but not my mother. She seemed to view my financially providing for myself as some form of disrespect toward her. It was also sad when

Momma would call me at work several times during my junior and senior years in high school and would beg me to go and spend the night with her mother when I got off work. By this time, Kenya was gone off to college and lo and behold the big bad wolf – Grandmomma San – was afraid to stay home alone at night. She had even gotten bars installed just for the front door.

My first thought was, *I should have made her call and ask me herself? Why should I be made to suffer through a night alone with her?* I would tell Momma yes, but only if she would agree to drop me off late and pick me up at the first sight of daybreak the very next morning. I would go over there and go straight to bed anticipating the morning. I didn't understand what made Momma think leaving me there with Grandmomma San would make her feel any safer; because if someone did try to get in, I was not going to save her for trying to save myself. I always believed that she was afraid to stay alone because in addition to being so mean and hateful, she was also a coward.

Living with Momma and Randall was much better than living in Hell, but we had our issues just like any other typical household with two teenagers living there. Momma still continued beating me on a regular basis for breathing. She would pick up anything she could get her hands on; a coax cable, a shoe, a wire hanger, her fist or foot or just take the palm of her hand to slap my face to the point of it vibrating.

One incident in particular – I remember it as if it were yesterday – my first cousin Kelvin, and his girlfriend Keshena, had a newborn baby girl and we were all visiting at Grandmomma San's house. I remember sitting in the living room with a room full of other relatives.

Well, Momma asked me to change the baby's diaper and of course I didn't want to because it was not my responsibility. I jokingly leaned over and whispered to Momma that the baby's dad, my cousin Kelvin, and her grandmother – my Aunt Sydney were there; insinuating that one of them should change the baby's diaper, which made sense to me anyway!

Momma loved to put on a show for people all of the time, no matter who was present. She enjoyed publicly embarrassing us at school or anywhere else. But it seemed as if I was her favorite target when it came to clowning people. Momma always made me feel as though she was repulsed by my very existence and that I was a burden or thorn in her side concerning life in general. Needless to say, she slapped me dead in my face and instantly it was tingling and turned red from the burning sensation. She hit me so hard I nearly fell out of my chair. Of course, the room got quiet and to really show off, Momma began to cuss and loud talk me as she made me change the diaper anyway. Aunt Sydney was never as mean toward me as my other two aunts'; Sharon and Nachelle. She insisted that Kelvin change his own daughter's diaper, but Momma would not listen. It was her way of showing me and everyone else that she had the upper hand. Dishing out humiliation was a way of life for her as a parent. I think she enjoyed it and somehow felt empowered by belittling, degrading and criticizing her children.

My mother was not someone I could talk to; that's why we never really had a relationship as I was growing up. It was always her way or no way. She would never listen to me and I'd better not open my mouth to try and share my feelings with her or question any of her decisions or actions. She considered this talking back disrespectfully; and it was a quick way to get you slapped, cursed out or both. I constantly felt like her personal punching bag. I think the failure of her and my father's relationship caused her to take all of her other frustrations in life out on me at every opportunity she got.

Daddy wasn't any better than Momma when it came to raising children. Not only could I not communicate with him either, but he slapped my brother and me once just out of the clear blue. When we began to cry and look confused, his exact words were, "I slapped you because I can." His pride had set in and he wanted to prove to us in a very arrogant way that no matter what, he was always going to be our daddy; or it could have been just his plain old ignorance. He would always tell me that I was an accident and if it wasn't for Momma and me, he would not have missed out on going to college nor would he have messed up his entire life. Constantly, he reminded me that he was paying for the time I spent with him through his child support payments which were a measly $65.00 every two weeks. He used his payments as an excuse not to do anything else for me.

I remember him picking me up to take my older brother Alvin Jr. shopping for school clothes and supplies and I knew better than to ask for anything. Daddy made it very clear that he had only picked me up to show me what he was buying for my brother because *his* mother had not put him on child support like mine had. I thought parents were supposed to support you emotionally, academically, physically, spiritually and...financially! This did not help the ill feelings I already had toward my brother.

My big brother would also hump and fondle me when he and I were at Grandmomma Emily's on some weekends. So, not only did I have to deal with A.B. at home, I had to fight off my half-brother on the weekends. He was four years older than me, but apparently, he had been exposed to sex and tried to not only get me to perform oral sex on him at age six, but to do sexual favors for his friends from across the street as well.

I was too afraid to service him or his friends and I told him I didn't want to get pregnant. It's sad that at the age of six, I already knew what sex was and the repercussions that could come from it. As we got older, I began to avoid being around Alvin Jr. as much as possible. He had already assured me that when I turned fifteen he was going to rape me. Of course we grew apart as the years went by. He was a teenager and didn't come over as much as he had before, and eventually, I forgave him and realized that his threats were just crazy babblings of a ten year old at the time.

I'm thankful that I was able to truly forgive Alvin Jr., because now as we are adults, we're closer than we ever were before. I was truly able to release my anger for him after I broke down in tears when I was seventeen and told Momma what he had done to me.

At that time, Alvin Jr. really wasn't a threat because I didn't see him often. I only got to see him when Daddy brought us all together for the annual Nixon Family Reunion or for vacation. On those occasions, Daddy would always let me know if we went on a vacation together that the only reason I could come along was to help him with his girlfriend's younger children and I was only in his Will because my younger sister, Bridgette, was not old enough to be in it. He even told me once that he could not allow himself to get close to me because I was a girl.

To which I replied, "That doesn't make sense because as a girl, I am still close to: Randall, Uncle Curtis, Uncle James, and Uncle Randy; they have always looked out for me and were protective." I could go on and on about the things Daddy said, but after a while, I guess I just became numb to all of Daddy's negative comments. Even Grandpa Howard had more compassion for me than Daddy did. I just never understood how his own dad could love me more than he did as my father.

It was hard to understand how Daddy, Grandmomma Emily and Grandpa Howard were cut from the same cloth. His heart was so different from theirs toward his own children. I think Momma still has Daddy's heart to some extent, because he could never see me or talk to me on the phone without mentioning Momma and the negativity of their past together. It was as if he wanted me to do something about it; like he wanted me to somehow change the past. He would always say that I loved her more than I loved him and that was far from the truth. I was not trying to be on either of their sides nor in the middle of their messy past.

After a while, I stopped trying to establish a relationship with Momma or Daddy. I eventually built up walls around myself to protect my heart from any more pain and disappointment. What kept my head above water – along with my faith in Jesus Christ – was that I knew and would often say, "He didn't bring me this far to leave me," not knowing, at the time, that I was sowing seeds and speaking my future into existence. I always knew that someday God would deliver me from such a negative and cruel environment. No matter how many times I tried to guard my heart and just accept that my parents did not want to be a part of my life and just be done with them, the Holy Spirit would always convict me to make peace and to keep praying for my parents. In the meantime, since I wasn't getting the love, support and guidance I needed as a child, naturally – out of my own ignorance – I began to look for it elsewhere; and in all of the wrong places.

It seemed as if after I finally told Momma about being molested by A.B., I started having sex. Later, I kind of wished I had not told her so my fear and thoughts of A.B. could have saved me from being sexually active at such a young age. Monique and I were reunited around the time I entered high school. . Her mom actually moved to Dallas and coincidentally, she began dating one of Momma's cousins who she ended up marrying. I was thrilled to have the two of them back in my life because Katelyn had always treated me like her daughter as well.

Monique and I had missed out on so much time together and had a lot of catching up to do. We would talk on the phone for hours and try to get to each other's house every weekend. One day during our catching up sessions, she lied and told me that she had already had sex. Like a dummy, I tried it so that I could keep up with her and after I told her what I had done, she said, "Girl! I was just playing!" Well, it was too late then because I was serious. I was in and out of so many relationships at the time that it was pitiful. I dated guys that slept with guns underneath their mattresses, who sold drugs, did credit card fraud, gambled and only God knows what else.

I never participated in any of their activities, but being so young and naïve...I could care less what they were doing. All I could see was how they were treating me and I thought, at the time, that they actually loved me. This line of thinking on my part was a result of being misguided and growing up in an environment where this was the norm since both of my parents were going through a variety of relationships on their own throughout my childhood. Not to mention the fact that I had also overheard Kenya on the phone talking about having sex, so my curiosity lead me down a path of regrets.

Momma would often leave us home alone; sometimes for a couple of days at a time without any groceries. Kenya would come to visit some weekends, and on one of these occasions she had a friend over with her. We were all so hungry that we took corn, green beans and everything else we could find in the fridge or the pantry and mixed it together for lunch. We were practically raising ourselves and acting like adults way before our time. As a matter of fact, Kenya was in our townhouse one weekend alone. I was at Monique's and Teresa was away visiting her Dad in East Texas. Kenya's boyfriend, the very popular Casey G., came by. Momma had left for the club, but returned home because she'd forgotten her ID. Kenya and Casey had dead bolted the front and back door because they were having sex on the living room floor. Panicking and hearing Momma pounding and screaming for someone to open the door, Casey grabbed his clothes and ran upstairs to hide. He was butt naked and hoping that she would not find him in the closet in me and Teresa's bedroom. Kenya finally opened the door wearing Momma's robe.

"What took you so long to open the door?" Momma yelled, eyeing her suspiciously.

"I was getting in the shower," Kenya replied, sounding a little out of breath.

Our townhouse was not that big and there was one small guest restroom on the first floor. When Momma came in, the only light that was on was coming from the small restroom on the first floor and as Kenya headed up the stairs, Momma decided to turn the light off before going up to her room to retrieve her ID for the club. To her dismay, as she reached in to turn the light off, she looked down and saw a condom floating in the toilet. She screamed for Kenya and asked who else was in the house. I'm not sure if Kenya lied or fessed up, but Momma found Casey hiding in the closet and put him out of the house, but not before threatening to throw both Casey and Kenya from the second story window.

Shortly thereafter, Momma's youngest sister, Nachelle, took me and Kenya to the doctor's office to start us on birth control pills. I remember Momma being so upset that she took away the free condoms that we had gotten from the doctor. I had no true concept of the fact that sex was something special to be shared once you were married; but instead of Momma explaining this to me, she would always talk around it or change the subject whenever someone else would bring it up. Her infamous explanation was, "It's nasty, just don't do it!" That was it. I never got much more out of her on the subject.

Without getting much out of Momma about how relationships should work, I was often confused about sex and how to interact with boys. After having sexual intercourse with a boy, our relationship would end almost immediately. This wasn't always because of them, but often had to do with me as well. It was sad that I endured one heartbreak after another; yet I kept going around the same stupid mountain getting nowhere fast. Thankfully, I didn't have sex in every relationship I was in, but I didn't know the first thing about loving anyone or allowing them to love me. I ended up breaking off most of my relationships out of fear of trusting the other person and due to feelings of inadequacy. I would find one reason or another to bring my relationships to an end. You would have thought I would have stopped and told myself that I had had enough of being hurt and used; but I truly thought that if I kept giving myself and my heart to these boys, that one day I would meet one who really loved me. Boy was I wrong; they all wanted the same thing and none of them ever loved me.

It had gotten so bad that in one relationship, I actually had a good Christian boyfriend that went to another school across town. We dated for two years when I ended up taking his virginity and then leaving him for an older guy who meant me no earthly good. The guy I left my boyfriend for participated in some illegal activities and had lots of money, a house and three or four cars. Since I was trying to get away from Momma's house by any means necessary, I thought that by getting involved with the older guy, he would be willing to help me move out of Momma's house. But of course the relationship did not last!

After a few years of ups and downs in one bad relationship after another, my self-worth and self-esteem were very low. I felt dispensable, unloved and just down right lost! I had no visions, plans or goals for the future. I didn't know which way to go or what to do with my life; if I had known then what I know now, I could have saved myself a lot of heartache, confusion and unnecessary pain. I had become wrapped up in a vicious cycle, and Satan was having a field day continuing to set up stronghold after stronghold in my mind. Sometimes I didn't know which way to turn.

As I mentioned earlier, I had accepted Jesus Christ as my personal Savior in 1991 while attending church with my Grandmother Emily; but being a teenager and so hooked on boys, I didn't visit her as often as I had as a child. Therefore, I was not in church every weekend like I was before. Momma very rarely went to church; but she would sometimes send us with someone else or drop us off and speed away. I didn't learn how to truly fellowship, develop a relationship, or how to live for God until I was a young adult, and like with most things in life, I learned that on my own. But I had watched Grandmomma Emily read her Bible every morning that I woke up at her house as a child and we shared a great deal of wonderful times together. Watching her connect with God every morning is a vision that still lingers in my mind. I will always remember our weekly garage sales and her making me mayonnaise sandwiches. My grandmother would use this time to impart wisdom and share with me how much God loves me. She was the backbone and fabric of everything that is good in my life. Had it not been for Grandmomma Emily's guidance and love, I tremble just at the thought of where I may have ended up in life.

Whenever I had a problem or a question about sex or boys, I couldn't talk to Daddy or Momma so I would go to Grandmomma Emily or to my friends who didn't know any more than I did. It's not hard to imagine how much more trouble I got myself into by listening to my peers. I would sometimes talk to their parents, who I also referred to as Momma and Daddy because I saw the difference in the relationship that my friends had with their parents, versus the lack thereof with my own. I learned later that that type of association, in itself, is a cry for help and often occurs when either the presence of your own parents is nonexistent, or you simply don't have a proper relationship with them.

My junior year in high school was an awesome turning point and an unforgettable experience. I joined a Christian organization—The Alpha and Omega Angels. Tina Ford and Richard Triggs were the directors of our S.T.E.P. group, and they taught me so much about Christianity, values, choices and life that I'm able to cherish for a life time. I had been running track since the fourth grade and stopped running and joined the Maurine F. Bailey Concert Choir – a world-renowned organization. Mr. A. Jones was our director and I am also eternally grateful for the Christian impact that he had on my life as well. Being a part of these two very wonderful organizations changed my life and reminded me of the love of Jesus that I was introduced to by a stranger sitting on a pew next to me one Sunday morning. I shall never forget the powwows, the tears shed, the sound of laughter or the life lessons I learned from both of them.. These experiences gave me real focus and drive. They taught me the importance of reading my Bible more and having personal praise and worship time with God.

In 1998, I graduated with honors from Lincoln Humanities/Communications Magnet High School in Dallas, Texas. Yes, the same high school that Chris Bosh of the Miami Heat had attended! Upon graduation, I knew my prayers had finally been answered. I was so happy to be eighteen, leaving home and going off to college. My hopes to get as far away as possible had finally come true; or so I thought. It was a very exciting time in my life and things were going good. I packed all my things two whole months in advance. Our choir had gone to a competition in Waikiki, Hawaii and won first place. While there, I'd found $200 on the street in front of The Beachcomber Hotel where we were staying. I needed that money; it gave me the foundation I needed to start my new life. I used it for the deposit on my first apartment for college. It came in handy, especially after I returned home from Hawaii to learn that Momma had stolen $600 from my safe while I was away and said she had to pay some bills with it. She knew I'd been working hard and saving that money for months and needed it for books, food and housing. I was hurt; but more so, I was at a complete loss because I knew she had no remorse for having taken it, and I also knew that she would never pay me back. Out of all the things Momma had done to me…stealing my money when I needed it most was a new low…even for her.

I attended Texas Southern University in Houston, Texas for a very brief moment and ended up returning home. I had made the very costly mistake of rooming with friends I had known from junior high and high school and it did not work out very well at all. I quickly realized that I had left home for all of the wrong reasons. It wasn't that I was so excited about going off to college, but I was just trying to get away from Momma and Daddy. I tried several times to go back to college and even enrolled in some different schools shortly after I left, but going back to school just wasn't for me. I still have some family members that to this day comment on my leaving college; but of course, the comments come from the ones that did not go to college themselves. It's kind of funny how those that never took a leap of faith always have something to say to those that do.

When I wasn't able to stay in school, I did what a lot of people my age do when going to college doesn't work out. I moved back home and eventually got a job.

Lord knows this was the wrong move.

CHAPTER FOUR

Pregnant, Confused and Homeless

Honestly, while writing this, I wanted to skip this chapter of my life for fear of ridicule and judgment. But God helped me to realize that I couldn't if I wanted to truly convey the whole story; plus, you can never mix fear and faith together. By doing so, you give more weight to the wrong one. So I stepped out on faith to write this book; trying to ensure that God could truly get all of the glory. This portion of my life is just as important as every other part in making me who I am. It's a part of my life that even though it was quite bad, it helped me to finally change for the better. I was at a turning point in my life and it was then that I became a totally different person.

Leaving Texas Southern University was not the hard part. The hardest part about leaving school was that I had to go back and live with Momma. That was the part that I dreaded the most. Needless to say, I did and it did not take very long for things to return to the normal negativity that coursed through my life on a daily basis. The cursing, yelling and hitting began almost instantly once I stepped through the front door. I think that deep down inside of her, she was happy that I had finally left home, and that she thought, like I did, that I would not be coming back or at least not so soon.

After a few weeks rolled by, I began working at Kinko's and enrolled in school again at the Court Reporting Institute of Dallas. It was right down the street, which was awesome because I didn't have very far to go to catch the bus to work after school. Getting up at 4:00 a.m. and walking half a mile to the nearest bus stop to catch four buses to be on time by 7:00 a.m. was not an easy task; but I had to do whatever it took. I was actually doing very well at school, and being able to work and go to school allowed me to spend as little time as possible at home; which was great. I even found myself volunteering for overtime just to keep from going home.

For the first time ever, I felt focused and thought I knew where my life was headed. Everything seemed to be looking up for me until one day I came in to work and the first thing I heard from an unfamiliar voice saying, "Good Morning, Miss Lady! How are you?" I ignored him, clocked in and continued putting on my work apron and prepping my cash register. Finally, my boss Steve walked over to me and introduced a new coworker.

"I want you to meet our new sales rep, Rodney Hall," he said.

A tall, well-dressed and articulate brother who had manicured nails and pearly white teeth was the unfamiliar voice that I'd ignored at the start of my shift. He was what my girls and I liked to call a basketball body.

"Good morning, nice to meet you," Rodney said.

"Likewise," I mumbled and went back to working.

Instantaneously, Rodney became very popular around our store. He was always walking around with his head up like a lion full of pride. He always wore a shirt and necktie, along with elephant leg slacks and dress shoes. But what I remember most about him in the beginning was that he was always quoting the Bible and being very personable with everyone he came into contact with. He even spoke with a fake New Yorker's accent. Come to find out, this Negro was straight out of South Dallas just like me. I would look at him in the same manner that a cheetah prowls for prey, if only I had kept doing so.

He would pursue me every day, without fail; trying to strike up a conversation and inviting me out on dates. I kept telling him no and trying to avoid him. This was very difficult because I had to see his face every time I came to work and if that wasn't enough, we had the same lunch hour, so we were always on break at the same time. I knew there was something about him, but I just couldn't put my finger on it. I was also not interested in him because he was twenty-two – or at least that's what he told me at first – and I was only eighteen. I had never dated a guy that much older than me.

Rodney Hall could do what we called at the time – spit game; and he could do it like no one I have ever met before in my life. He was a smooth talker and surprisingly seemed to also be a good listener. If he wasn't a good listener, he sure knew how to fake like he was. He could be as smooth as a cat and yet as sneaky and deceptive as a snake.

There was a sitting area inside Kinko's where I went most days on my lunch to do my written assignments for school. One day, as I was sitting there quietly by myself as usual and I heard weeping coming from the direction of the restrooms not too far from where I was seated. At first, I ignored it and then I wondered who it could be? It sounded like it was coming from the men's restroom. As I sat there, the door finally swung open and there was Rodney with bloodshot red eyes sniffling and holding a fist full of tissue paper.

"What's wrong?" I asked out of concern.

He picked his big head up and smiled and said, "I knew you cared about me; all along you've just been playing hard to get."

"Never mind," I said, dreading that I had even asked.

I then quickly turned my attention back to my homework and he invited himself to take the seat across from me.

"No, but seriously...it's my Big Momma," he said. "She's sick and it's not looking very good. Man, if something ever happened to her, I don't know what I would do. I'd probably just die. My momma is a crackhead and my father never wanted anything to do with me, so I was raised by Big Momma."

I sat there as he ended up taking up the rest of my lunch break. Somehow we began talking about church and the Bible and one conversation lead to another and another. *This guy seems to be alright after all,* I said to myself.

Eventually, Rodney convinced me to go out on a date with him on a Saturday that he and I both had off from work. We would hang out all of the time and before I knew it, we were like each other's shadow. We had to see each other every day. After we had been dating a while, he began talking about marriage and what he wanted out of life; which I found out later was all just talk. I should have read all of the signs; he was really a twenty-six-year-old-man living with his aunt. He had two daughters and two baby mamas and the car he drove was only available a few days a week, which turned out to belong to another girl he was dating. Sometimes we would have to catch the bus. Being so young and naïve, Rodney took full advantage of me and I was too stuck on him to see the situation for what it really was.

As the months rolled on, one day a customer walked up to my register and requested an order of flyers. The original read, *Now hiring extras for the movie, Any Given Sunday to be shot here in Dallas.* I thought about doing it for a split second for the extra money, but there was no way my schedule would have permitted it. As I was placing the customer's order, I noticed that he kept staring at me very intently.

Finally he asked, "Have you ever thought about becoming a model?"

"Sure," I answered right away, "but every time I've ever tried, it turned out to be a big money scam. I've paid money, had my profile shots taken and traveled before to modeling competitions and they always turned out to be bogus."

"Well, you should really reconsider it," he said. "I can put you in contact with a very good friend of mine that owns the El Roy Roberts Modeling Agency in Ft. Worth. Here's my card, give me a call when you've had a chance to think about it."

"Thank you," I said. "But I can tell you right now that I am very interested!"

"Great, then I'll be in touch. We can go over some of the details here at the end of your shift if you like."

"Okay cool," I said. I was so excited.

"Quee, come here," said Rodney. He was the only person in the world that called me Quee and not Nikki!

"I can't leave my register," I said. "You come over here."

Rodney was skeptical of this man from the start. He immediately ran over to my register to be nosey.

"Who was that cat?" he asked.

"Just some kind of talent scout," I said. "Don't trip...it ain't deep."

"Well, he sure had you smiling and talking for a long time," scolding me as if he were my father.

"You're just jealous" I said. "As good looking as that man was, he was not trying to holler at me. He was hooking me up with some fly connections though. When he comes back to pick up this order of flyers we're going to talk some more."

"Oh! Really! Is that right?" he said in an aggravated tone.

"Yeah, that's right and if it's that crucial for you, you can join us."

"Well, I think I just may have to do that. You don't know this man from Adam; he could be a smooth talking rapist or psycho killer; you never know. You can't just leave yourself open baby girl. I'm telling you Quee...older cats will try to take advantage of a sweet, young, pretty, yellow bone like you."

Tell me about it, I thought to myself, still blind to the fact that he had just described himself.

Later that afternoon, Paul – the talent scout – returned about twenty minutes before closing. We weren't busy that late in the day because the customer rush had already passed. So Rodney and I went over to meet with him. Before I could open my mouth to introduce the two of them to each other, Rodney introduced himself and began to bombard the man with a lot of questions. Paul answered all of Rodney's questions and everything sounded awesome and legit; but I was never the type of person to get hyped up about something great...that is until it actually happened to me. The first thing Paul said after his twenty question interview with this idiot was, "Nikki, I spoke with my friend over at El Roy Roberts about you earlier today. He said it would be great if we could set up a time to meet with you and your parents because you're under twenty-one, so we have to have their permission to work with you."

"That's fine. I'll talk to them about it tonight when I get home," I said, all the while thinking to myself that I could understand talking to my step-dad Randall, but I knew that given the fact that Momma was always so negative and would tell me how stupid I was and how I would never be anything but a troublemaker, I could foresee her shooting this dream down before it could ever lift off.

The following week, Paul came over to my house to meet my parents and to pick up my headshots. Momma and Randall sat curiously and listened to Paul. He explained to my parents that the El Roy Roberts Agency was willing to give me a modeling contract and that I would have to move to Los Angeles soon. He was able to answer all of their questions and put them at ease. We sat there talking for what seemed like forever and Paul even coached me on my posture, how to walk correctly and how I needed to dress when we went to the modeling agency.

A few days later, my parents allowed Paul to take me to Ft. Worth to meet the agents at the El Roy Roberts Agency. Everyone there liked me and we were ready to finalize the process of the contract but there was just one more requirement…I had to get a full physical before the contract could be completed.

"No problem," I said. "I'll make the appointment as soon as possible."

For as long as I can remember, I've dreamed of becoming a model and an actress. The opportunity to model had never presented itself before now and I was extremely excited. I couldn't wait to set the wheels of my dream into motion. I went to the doctor that Tuesday afternoon. After my physical was over, my doctor came back into the room and she said, "I can't sign off on the sheet you brought me. One of the stipulations of the requested physical was to make sure that you weren't pregnant. Well, I need to inform you that you're nine weeks pregnant."

"No, not me," I said. "There has to be some sort of mix up. You must have picked up the wrong test," I practically yelled.

I argued with her so much that she agreed to give me another test and she even let me see her do it and wait for the results. As she took the dropper from my urine sample and dropped the urine onto the test, my body felt numb. I had never been so nervous before in my life. The two pink lines appeared in the box again, indicating to be positive for pregnant. I was so confused. I just sat there like a deer caught in head lights with my mouth wide open and my contract crushed.

"Momma is going to kill me," I cried out. "I don't understand how this could have happened. I've been taking the birth control pills that Auntie Nachelle had put me on for three and a half years now."

I mean…I knew that I would accidentally forget and miss one or two occasionally, but I thought it took years for the pill to get out of your system before you could get pregnant. This myth was obviously not true at all.

"What am I going to do?" I said, looking into the doctor's eyes.

"Well," said Doctor Patel, "were you using the condoms that I gave you? Have you been having unprotected sex?"

"No, I haven't been using the ones that you gave me because Momma always gets upset and takes them; but Rodney and I always use a condom."

She tried to calm me down as we walked down the hall and into her office. She explained my options and began giving me pamphlet after pamphlet on various pregnancy options from having the baby and keeping it, to adoption and abortion. Honestly, I was so afraid my mind began to race and I could not focus on what she was saying. I was thinking to myself that I didn't know what I was going to do and to top it off, my oldest sister Kenya had just had her first baby the day before. I had told everyone about my modeling contract and about moving to LA. *Now what was I going to do?* I was the main one out of all of my friends who said I would never have any children. I guess we shouldn't be so quick to say what we will never do.

The pregnancy did explain why I had been vomiting and feeling so fatigued. I just thought I had a stomach virus or something. I had even started eating more junk food than usual, but I hadn't paid much attention to it. Before I went to the doctor I had talked to Monique about my cycle being late and explained that it had never been late before. She said not to panic and it could have been caused by stress and me being under a lot of pressure at the time. Boy was I in for more than what I thought.

I took my sack of pamphlets off of Doctor Patel's desk as she wrote down my next scheduled appointment for the nurse. Then I rode the bus to Grandmomma San's house where Momma and everyone else was. Kenya had dropped out of college and was living with Grandmomma San at the time, so our family was over there visiting her and her new baby girl.

I had put a lot of goodies inside the sack with the pamphlets from my doctor on the ride home. I still didn't know what to do, who to tell, or if I should tell anyone. As soon as I walked in the front door and sat my stuff down, Momma asked me to run out to the car to get some of the gifts that my new niece had gotten at the hospital.

"Yes ma'am," I said and got her keys and went back out of the front door. As I was walking out of the door, Auntie Nachelle asked me what I was eating and I told her I had a bag full of candy and gum in my sack...forgetting all about the pamphlets and the doctor's notes. I went out to the car and began to bring the gifts inside. When I was just about done bringing them in, I noticed my Auntie and Momma whispering.

"Come here for a minute, Nikki...when you get through," they said.

When I walked back in the door it still had not dawned on me that they had been in my sack.

"Where did y'all go?" I said out loud, looking for the two of them.

"We're in the kitchen," said Auntie Nachelle.

As I walked into the kitchen, she and Momma were standing next to the washer and dryer and out of all of the pamphlets in my sack, the one Momma was holding in her hand was the one about abortion.

"Are you pregnant?" Auntie Nachelle asked.

I paused in fear of being knocked to the floor and looked at Momma trying to read her facial expressions, but she just looked confused and caught by surprise.

"Are you?" Auntie Nachelle asked again.

"Yes," I said.

To my complete amazement, Momma's exact words were, "That's okay, you've graduated from school; you're grown and you like to keep a job...so I know you'll take care of it. If you get an abortion though, I will never speak to you again."

"I wasn't going to get an abortion. Doctor Patel was just giving me all of my options."

Before we could finish hugging, my auntie blurted out to everyone else in the house, "Hey y'all, guess what...Nikki's pregnant!"

Grandmomma San yelled, "WHAT!" in awe, as if my baby was going to be her responsibility or something.

As soon as I got home that evening, I tried calling Rodney to tell him the news, but there was no answer. He finally returned my call a few hours later.

"Hello," I answered.

"What's up, Quee? What are you doing?"

"Nothing, I need you to come through and pick me up. I have something to tell you."

"I can't right now, my aunt is gone in the car. What is it about?"

"Us," I said.

"Well, what is it?"

"I don't want to tell you over the phone?"

"Why? Is your momma listening on the other end?"

"No, I don't think so, but it wouldn't matter if she was because she already knows."

"Knows what, pretty girl?"

"I'll tell you when I see you in the morning, I'm going to sleep."

"I love you!" he said.

"Sure you do, bye," I said as I hung up the phone in the middle of his next sentence. I knew he probably thought I was upset at him for some reason, but I don't think he ever had a clue about what was really going on.

When I arrived at work the very next morning, he nearly knocked me down running up to me as I came through the front entrance.

"Man, what was up with you last night?" he asked.

"Stop talking all loud and come to the back with me to clock in. Why are you so crunk this early in the morning?"

"Quee what's up?" he yelled.

"I'm pregnant and my modeling contract is void. Are you happy now?"

"What do you mean 'am I happy now'?"

"You were jealous of my opportunity to move away and become a model from day one. All you could think about was yourself. I can kiss my dreams of a *Covergirl* commercial goodbye."

"That has nothing to do with anything" he said. "I wanted that for you...but I didn't want you to have to leave me to get it or for you to get hurt in the process. What are you going to do about this baby situation though?"

"What do you mean what am I going to do about it? Don't you mean what are *we* going to do about it?"

"No. I think *we* should go half on an abortion. I had been slipping the condom off from time to time because you felt so good; and plus, I thought you were on the pill. I wanted you to have my baby one day, but I never thought it would happen this soon."

"I am on the pill, you idiot, but if I miss one I could very easily get pregnant. Besides, the pill does not guarantee you will not get pregnant or even get an STD for that matter. You had no right to do that!" I yelled as I burst into tears.

I can't disclose the content of my next statement due to the extreme vulgarity and my maturity level at the time, but anyone who really knows me can probably imagine me telling him off. In other words, I let him have it. After reading him...I very kindly looked him right into his eyes and said, "I don't need you. *MY* baby and I will be just fine without you!"

Ever since I said those words, God has allowed that to be the truest statement I've ever uttered.

Needless to say, my boss, some coworkers and most importantly, some customers overheard our altercation and I was terminated at the end of my shift. That public display of foolishness really put the icing on the cake for my boss because he wasn't impressed with my attitude and attendance already. Rodney, on the other hand, was not fired. We did not call one another for weeks and then one day out of the blue, he was standing on the steps as I was leaving school to catch the bus home.

"What do you want?" I said.

"What do you mean, *what do I want*? Aren't you happy to see me?

I came to give you a ride home so you wouldn't have to catch the bus."

"No, you came to see if I would give you some."

"Come on, Quee…you know I love you; and besides, I miss that pretty face of yours."

"Well, that does not change the fact that I am pregnant with your baby and you don't want anything to do with me."

"I told you I would help you get rid of it and then we could be together again."

"Are you some kind of fool or what?" I asked. "I said *we* didn't need you and I meant that! As far as I am concerned, we don't have anything else to say to one another."

"Alright…cool," he said. "You'll need me long before I need you."

"You wish!" I yelled as I walked toward my bus stop. As he drove away staring at me, I gave him some rather rude and very apparent hand gestures as I yelled you *so and so* coward.

I tried to continue to go to school during my pregnancy, but walking that far to catch a bus by 4:00 a.m. carrying a stenograph machine was getting very hard as my belly got bigger. So, I ended up dropping out of school…AGAIN. I wanted a car so bad and I had been doing well saving my money in a safe Daddy had bought me one Christmas. I started looking for another job, but little did I know more hell was coming in my direction. Momma started ranting and raving about me being pregnant and not having any money to help with the bills. Eventually, the yelling she was doing wasn't quite enough in her eyes, and she couldn't hit me because I was pregnant, she decided to throw me out of her house. My life was in a downward spiral. I was pregnant, jobless and homeless.

I initially moved in with one of my Uncle James' ex-girlfriends, Aunt Sherry Body. She and I had been very close when I was growing up and even well into after they broke up. She was more like a friend to me than an adult figure. As a matter of fact, she used to sneak me out some times and take me to see Benny when he and I were dating. His uncle Demarcus worked downtown with her and she would either visit with him when Benny and I were spending time together, or she would leave me with Benny and then come back hours later to pick me up.

Anyway, I called her crying when Momma said I had to leave and she immediately came and picked me and all of my belongings up without hesitation. Momma had always been jealous of the friendship Aunt Sherry and I had and when she came to get me my Momma asked her, "Why would you let her come and live off of you?"

Aunt Sherry tried talking to Momma and telling her how much I needed my mother and that this was not the time to give up on me; but as usual, Momma didn't listen and she slammed the front door in both of our faces.

I went to live with Aunt Sherry for about a month and a half. To make a long story short...she met a younger man and he moved in. It was very apparent he wanted me out of the house, so I made sure she didn't have to ask me to leave. I tried to go back to Momma's house, but she would not let me come there. This just added to the discord between me and her. She had planted so many bad seeds in our relationship that a friendship seemed impossible; and no one wants to feel unimportant to their own mother. I ended up moving in with one of my closest childhood friends – Tenishia Crockett, her son, her siblings and her parents. Even though it was crowded there, it was the only place I had left to go.

I had been at Tenishia's place for about two weeks when my money, clothes and shoes started coming up missing. I had a brand new pair of Nike Airmax with the $130 receipt still in the box because I was going to return them. Well, let's just say someone beat me to it. Her mom had been trying to convince me to get an abortion from the day I moved in. One day I overheard her complaining to Tenishia's dad about the household bills and that my being there was costing them extra money for water, lights and groceries. They fought and yelled for over an hour; he was defending me and she wanted me gone. I felt pregnant, lonely, out of place and worried about where my next meal would be coming from and where I would be spending the night. It was sad that I had family, but I didn't feel I could have gone to live with any of them and I didn't want to become a financial burden on Grandmomma Emily.

I panicked and started searching the Yellow Pages and calling to check local shelters. I finally found one on Cadiz Street in downtown Dallas, but the beds were first come, first serve and by the time Tenishia and her dad helped me pack up all of my things and we went down there, there was no room for me. Her dad begged her mom to let me stay until I could find somewhere else to go. I ended up moving from one friend's house to another until all of the money I had saved and half of my clothes, shoes and other personal belongings were gone, either from being stolen or just left behind as I constantly moved.

If Momma got wind of where I was, she would even go as far as calling my friends' parents telling them to put me out on the streets to fend for myself. I felt betrayed, worthless and unloved. I had never felt so depressed and low in my entire life. I sometimes would cry and wonder *why am I still alive?* But, my God had a plan and He kept me in the midst of it all. Finally Katelyn – Monique's mom – came to Dallas to pick me up. She took me in with no problem. She helped me get a job, enrolled me into a prenatal care program and had Monique and I very active in their church. I had gotten in contact with Rodney when I was about four months pregnant and Katelyn would not allow me to see him. It was a good thing she didn't because his attitude was the same as when I left so it was for the best. He acted as if he was so concerned about all that I was going through, and yet he still never offered any help...not once!

When I was about seven and a half month's pregnant, Katelyn called Momma. The only thing I really remember her telling her was that this was her grandbaby and that she should want to be there for me when I give birth. I guess Momma agreed and there I was...moving back to Dallas. I don't know if Momma let me come back out of guilt, sympathy or curiosity; but either way, she had not changed her bitter attitude toward me. She made sure I was very uncomfortable being there. Here I was getting ready to have my baby girl at any time, and she would fuss about me lying down in the bed for a nap during the day.

I had never liked being anywhere I was not welcomed. To try and avoid confrontation, if I got tired I would just lie down on the floor next to the bed and she wasn't happy with that either. She thought I was being sarcastic, but really I was just trying to do whatever it took to keep the peace. I realized that even with the arrival of my baby soon approaching, I would still not be able to stay there long.

One day, I walked down the street about half of a mile away to the Lake June Village Apartments which were low income so I was a shoe in. I wouldn't have much rent to pay and it was on the bus line. I immediately begged the owner to put me on the waiting list. Coincidently, when Momma took me back up there to turn in my application, the owner was an old classmate of hers from junior high and God showed me favor. She moved me up on the waiting list and guaranteed me an apartment within a month or so. I was so happy and thankful that I didn't know what to do except praise God and anticipate the count down.

I started packing immediately and marking off the days on my calendar with X's. It was at this time in my life that I found myself more and more engaged in my Bible and I knew that as I drew closer to God, He would draw closer to me. Randall would see me reading the Bible all of the time and he would encourage me to hang in there. That helped me more than he will ever know. I really wanted to be able to have a healthy relationship with Momma, and I dreamt of being allowed to just lay my head in her lap and cry as she encouraged me and gave me guidance. But that dream was one she was not interested in.

My due date was Thanksgiving of 1999, but on November 14th, the day after my baby shower, I delivered a six pound, seven ounce baby girl; I named her Miracle Nixon. She was the most beautiful little person I had ever laid my eyes on. She was me made over. Our baby and toddler pictures look exactly the same. So much so, that sometimes she doesn't believe me when I show her a picture of me as a little girl; she swears it's her and not me. Children seem to think that we came into the world as adults and could never have been small.

I brought her home from the hospital and back to Momma's house when she was about two days old and I loved on her and cherished her so. I was very protective of her. I remember some nights reading the Bible to her and telling her stories as if she was a big girl. I would even hold up items with bright colors just to see her little head turn to try and focus on them. She would naturally keep me up a lot during the night. Sometimes I would let her sleep on my chest because she seemed to sleep for longer periods of time in that position.

I remember being so tired and sitting at the edge of the bed trying to rock her to sleep and falling asleep myself; nodding in and out. One night I did that and Momma opened the door to my room and she took her from me and accused me of being drunk when she saw that I was dozing off. I had never been drunk before in my life; but it was sad that she didn't know this or felt that I would do something so irresponsible. I thought it was ridiculous for her to see me trying to do the right things and yet she kept trying to pull me down and make me out to be a bad horrible person. She was always gossiping about me and slandering my reputation to her friends and family over the phone. It was like the more God blessed me to prove her wrong, the meaner she got.

She was so happy that Rodney was not there for me and the baby, so she could say *I told you so* a thousand times a day. She never liked him anyway because he was older than I was, and she called him loud and obnoxious every time she talked about him. He liked to be the center of attention and that bugged Momma. He liked to joke around a lot and sing...*boy could he sing!* Now that I look back on it, that's probably the only good quality he has that I am aware of.

I was blessed with a job at a local bank in walking distance from Momma's house and actually right across the street from my future apartment complex. After working there for about a month and paying daycare, the owner called me to let me know that my apartment was available and ready for move-in. I was so ecstatic and overwhelmed with joy that I didn't know what to do with myself. I prayed to God and asked Him that once He allowed me to move away from my mother's house that He make it so that I would never have to go back to live there again. After all of these years, He's done just that!

There were so many nights that I didn't have food in the apartment, no money and no transportation. I would just make sure Miracle had everything she needed, and I just sacrificed my own needs and went hungry until I could make ends meet. I could not call Momma even though she was right up the street. She was already complaining about having to help get my baby back and forth to daycare, so I made it a point not to ask her for anything else...ever!

I eventually started working at the grocery store where my bank was located. I would clock out at the bank and put my apron on and clock in on the cash register. I had just about saved up enough money to purchase my first car. Rodney had heard through the grapevine that I had moved and had my own place. They say once you feed a stray cat be careful because he will come back for more. He was too much of a coward to come around my parents or any of my family once he decided he didn't want anything to do with me and the baby. He wouldn't even come to the hospital. When I was in labor, I called him and his exact words were, "What you telling me for," and he hung up the phone.

I had not heard from him since that day until one day, as I was home getting settled in my new place and two of my friends Quita Washington and Jay Phynon were there when he knocked at the door. I looked through the blinds and nearly blew a gasket.

"What are you doing here and who told you where I lived?" I yelled through the window. My friends had heard all about this trifling guy, but had never laid eyes on him until then. Quita looked him up and down as she opened the door to let him in. I just went and sat back down next to Jay on the couch.

"What's up, Quee?" he said.

"What do you mean, *what's up*? How did you know where to find us?"

"Don't worry about that," he said with a smirk.

"Unless you have some milk and pampers for me, I don't know why you wasted your energy tracking me down."

"What! I can't come see my baby?"

"Well, she's four months old now and she is *my* baby," I said in a stern voice. "The same one I called you to come visit at the hospital and the same baby that you have been telling everyone is not yours!"

We were all in the living room and Miracle was asleep in her crib. Quita and Jay asked if they needed to leave and I told them they could stay and they did for a little while longer; but eventually, they had to leave. I should have known once they walked out that Rodney was up to no good when he sat down and began meddling; not once asking where the baby was. His entire conversation was probing to try and figure out if I was seeing someone and what I had been up to for the last several months and he reeked of alcohol.

"None of that is your business and why do you care all of a sudden?" I asked. "What is it that you want?"

"I want to make things right. I want us to be a family. I am so sorry, pretty girl. I know I messed up."

"I don't want to be with you, but if you want to be a part of her life…you can," I said. "Are you really all of a sudden concerned about us or did you get the child support notification in the mail and decide you were going to come and try to talk me out of it? Well, you can't sweet talk and manipulate me this time. Or do you really think I can allow you to make a fool of me again? No, we can't be anything," I added.

He got up and moved from the chair to the couch where I was sitting and began crying and sobbing. *He was quite an actor!* I guess all of the yelling woke the baby and I ran into her room to get her. When I brought her out, he took one look at her for the very first time ever and said, "She looks just like me."

"How is that possible?" I asked. "You have been telling people she is not your baby."

"I never said that, Quee. Can I hold her?"

"Yes, but be careful."

He started sobbing and weeping again and singing to her. She was just looking around like...*what is going on and who are you?*

After I fed and changed Miracle, she went back to sleep and I took her to her crib again. I came back in the living room and Rodney was not there.

"Where are you?" I asked.

"I'm in here. I am in your room."

"Get out of my room," I said as I stormed from the living room. "It's time for you to go."

"No, Quee, I want us to be together again and if I can't have you... nobody can."

"Rodney, get out! I don't want you and there is nothing you can do to make me change my mind."

Well, let's just say he was one of those guys who was not used to hearing no. He picked me up and threw me on my bed. I was all of a hundred and fifteen pounds next to a two hundred and twenty pound muscular man.

"Get off of me!" I screamed. "I don't want you!"

He began kissing on me and ripping my shorts and panties off. Not only had Rodney left me before: pregnant, clueless and destitute, but he returned again to do more damage as if he had not done enough already. He forced his penis inside me and held me down as I lay there crying and defenseless. After he came, he got up out of the bed and walked toward the bathroom. I had tears running down my face. I could hear my baby crying as we had awakened her again from her nap and I imagine she was very frightened.

"Just get out!" I said.

He put his head down as if he realized at that moment what he had really just done was raped me, but he just could not bring himself to care.

"Forget you, Nikki I hate you," he said as he walked out of the door. "I thought you loved me."

He was still talking when I slammed the door in his face and locked it. I went into the bathroom and began to sob aloud. I felt like I had no one to call. *Who would even care that I had just been raped while my infant child lay screaming in the next room? Certainly not Daddy or Momma, so why would the police care*, I thought. A few weeks went by and lo and behold...I was pregnant by this fool again. I could not believe that after all I had been through and endured this too could happen to me. I was so afraid. I needed to get an abortion. I called Rodney for the money, but of course he was broke. I had to finally tell a friend and she gave me half of the money to get an abortion. There was no way I could have made it with two babies when I was barely scraping by with one. I remember sitting on the hallway floor some evenings so broke and hungry I could cry. Thank God for W.I.C. or

Miracle would not have had food either.

Chanique Dean and I have been best friends since 1985. We have been there for each other through numerous trials, this one included. I called to ask her to drive me to my appointment and she was there to support me without judgment. But having an abortion turned out to be one of the worst decisions I had ever made in my life. I asked Rodney to just be there at the appointment and he could not even do that! Although, I don't know what made me ask him to be there for the abortion when he couldn't find it in his heart to be there for the birth of our daughter, or to simply apologize for what he had done. But I asked him anyway, and when he didn't come, I regretted asking him in the first place.

As the doctor suctioned the unborn child from my womb, I could feel it and hear the tiny body being chopped up in the little bucket with the machine attached to it. Even under a low dosage of anesthesia, I was well aware of what was going on. I cried the entire time and my body shook violently on the operating table like a leaf on a tree blowing uncontrollably in a fierce wind.

It took me a great deal of time to get over the entire event. Mentally, it wore me down. I tried to put it out of my mind and just move on with my life, but I couldn't...not for a long time. I knew God could not be pleased with what I had done even under the circumstances in which I became pregnant. I was ashamed, lonely and afraid. *Is this going to continue to be my life story?* I wondered. I knew that God said He would never leave me nor forsake me and that He would never put more on me than I could bear. I also knew that He had not brought me this far through all I had faced and endured to turn away from me. This fact and my baby were all I had left to hold on for. What other family did I have besides her and Grandmomma Emily? None; they were all I had.

Sometimes over the years, I would regret the fact that I took a lot of my anger and frustration out on Miracle; as she got older, I had to catch myself to avoid it. She did not ask to be here. God gave her to me for a reason and I did not want to make the same mistakes with her as my mother had made with me. I came to that realization right after my first cousin, Kelvin, who was twenty-two at the time, died while at dinner in Joe's Crab Shack in Mesquite. My other cousin, Andrew, who was nineteen and the same age as I was, also committed suicide around the same time that Kelvin died. They were both only children in the scheme of things, and yet they were both dead. Both of their mothers were in deep sorrow. I was carrying a lot on my shoulders during that time and their deaths at such young ages were a huge wake up call for me. Life is not promised to any of us and it is too short to be taken for granted. I realized then that we should cherish our lives and the people in it.

I had finally saved just about enough money to buy my first car. Daddy put the last $600 that I was short on his credit card. He told me to pay him back as much as I could at a time…with interest. I was thankful that this was his first act of kindness toward me ; but honestly, I wondered why he felt I should have to pay him back anything. After all, he had not done anything for me in my entire life. *Why couldn't he do one thing for his daughter without it having strings attached?*

I was young, but became very independent. Working two part-time jobs was hard; but having to be away from Miracle so frequently was even harder. I finally resigned from both of the part-time jobs and got a steady full-time job at Optel Telecommunications as a Customer Service Representative. That's when I met what I thought was the man of my dreams.

CHAPTER FIVE

But now I see...or so I thought

When I started working at Optel, I met and befriended a very interesting acquaintance by the name of Carl Thompson. He and I had a strictly platonic and awesome friendship. He treated me as his little sister; and after a while, we became prayer partners. Coincidentally, Carl happened to be the godfather of two little boys that were fathered by Rodney Hall. In fact, that is how Carl and I met. I had pictures of Miracle on my desk and he had his godsons' pictures on his and noticed the resemblance one day as he was walking by. I should have known something was up when he asked me what Miracle's fathers name was. Come to find out, Rodney had six or more other children that I had no earthly idea existed. The only two I knew about were the two little girls I had seen on pictures at his aunt's house. He turned out to be a sociopathic professional liar and was not taking care of any of his children from many different mothers.

For several days as I sat in the break room, a tall, fine and handsome young man with beautiful light brown eyes and a caramel complexion would speak to me and try to get me to notice him. I would always ignore him and continue to watch my favorite show which aired every day just in time for my break. I had heard the name Hayden around the office before, but did not know that this was the same guy being mentioned. He had just recently been hired into the Optel's Telephone Department.

One afternoon, some of my coworkers were trying to get me to sing for them because Carl had mentioned to them that I could really sing after he had heard me singing over the phone one night after work.   Then Hayden Tatum III walked through the door. He came to tell his best friend, who just happened to be Carl, that he was getting ready to leave for the day.

"Okay man, I'll catch up with you later," Carl said.

I stopped singing and looked up at him as he was getting ready to walk out of the door and we caught each other's eye. He was already staring at me when I looked up.

"You two should hook up," Carl said aloud as if a light bulb had just appeared over his head. I don't think Hayden heard him.

But as soon as he left, I quickly let Carl know that I was not interested in having a relationship right now. "I have been through enough, but he is kind of cute," I said.

Needless to say, Carl later gave Hayden my number anyway and the first time he called, I very rudely blew him off. I told him that I couldn't talk because I was getting my hair braided and hung up. He called back once more later on that evening and I replied the same way; but that time, I added that I would call him back when I was done if it wasn't too late. I had just turned twenty at the time and was finally at a point where I did not care if I met another man in my life. I was very afraid to give anyone else the chance to break my heart again. I did not want a boyfriend or anything else of the sort.

After a while, when I was done getting my hair braided that night, I called him and we talked for hours as if we had known one another forever. He had reached a point in his life of being tired of one meaningless relationship after another and so had I. We talked on the phone almost every night for the first couple of weeks and emailed back and forth all day during work. We had become so drawn to one another and eventually he and I began to date. Ironically, the song, "How Did You Get Here" by Deborah Cox had just come out and it was like my theme song. In spite of that, we hit it off from our very first date. He and I would sometimes fall asleep on the phone and wake up the next morning still on the line. He was very active in church, well-mannered and respectable. He was a breath of fresh air to me concerning my track record with men.

I began going to visit his church every Sunday where his dad Hayden Tatum Jr. was the Pastor. I eventually joined his church. We would leave church and go to his parents' house for dinner every Sunday. His mom, Martha, was a great cook and she loved it when Miracle and I would come over. So much so, that eventually, she allowed us to start sleeping over at their house with Hayden in another room of course. Momma was not happy about our relationship when she found out.

She'd say, "What kind of Pastor would let you and Miracle spend the night in his house and you and Hayden aren't even married?"

I had concluded that telling her and my Daddy – Alvin – anything good was not a good idea because they were going to have something negative to say every time I opened my mouth. Martha and I had become so close that she would come and take Miracle to her checkups or pick us up to go shopping with her. She was very generous and would offer me money to help me out from time to time, no matter how many times I would decline. I was grateful that she always thought of us and I tried paying her back, but she would never allow it.

During that time in my life, I was still really a sad little girl on the inside. I was recovering from molestation, being unwanted and unloved by my own family, struggling for guidance and recently rape by my child's father. So to meet such wonderful, God-fearing people...I thought God had finally heard my prayers and saw that I deserved a better life and for people to love me and treat me with acceptance, kindness and respect. After all, if my life had gotten any worse after my experiences from the ages of five to twenty, I don't know if I could have stood to take much more. I had finally arrived and was happy to be welcomed!

Hayden was the only boy of four children. He had three older sisters; Mariah was the eldest and he also had twin sisters, Yolita and Charlotte. Mariah lived in Irving, Texas and was a little snooty and standoffish, so I didn't have much conversation for her at all. I had dealt with enough of that in my own family. Charlotte lived in Austin and would only visit on major holidays. Yolita and Hayden lived with their parents and since I visited so often, Yolita and I became very close. She was cool people; very laid back and honest. She and Hayden's entire family had quickly fallen in love with Miracle.

One morning while I was at work, two older women in their early forties came and sat their chairs behind me at my desk. I thought this was odd, but I kept on working thinking to myself, *maybe they're doing some sort of training exercise.* Then I heard one of them whisper, "That's Hayden's girlfriend, she thinks he's all hers," and they laughed and walked away. I asked my coworker, Kieona who they were and she said "That's Angel and Sherry, they work upstairs."

I emailed Hayden and asked him if he knew of them and he replied back saying, "Yes, I counsel with Angel all the time."

"Counsel her…how so?" I replied.

"Just giving her insight on the Bible and providing scriptures for her encouragement."

Not too long afterwards, Angel started prank calling my work phone and making snide remarks about me and Hayden and our relationship. After she harassed me for about three days straight, I told Hayden I didn't want to be with him anymore and then called Angel's extension from the break room phone and told her if she wanted him so bad she could have him.

He insisted that his interaction with her was innocent and that he had done nothing to disrespect me or our relationship. I told him that he had also done nothing to speak up for me or our relationship against her either and I walked away. He and I did not talk for three days and

I kept avoiding him at work. Then one evening as soon as Miracle and I walked in the door, my phone rang.

"Hello," I answered and Martha was on the line crying.

"Nikki, how are you?" she asked.

Puzzled...I replied, "I'm good. I'm just getting ready to bathe Miracle."

"Well, I just called to tell you that I don't know what happened between you and my son, but he loves you and whatever it is I don't care...it can be fixed."

I went on to explain to her that I had told Hayden in the beginning of our relationship that I didn't want to play any games or get my heart broken again.

"He came to me crying and said that the woman made it all up, so you should not believe her," she said. "Y'all need to sit down and talk. I'm cooking...you can come over here for dinner."

"Well, I don't know if that's a good idea," I said.

But she insisted by saying that if she didn't know anything else, she knew that Hayden loved me and we needed to work this out. So, when Miracle and I were done with our baths, we got dressed and headed to Duncanville.

Hayden was sitting on the couch talking to his dad when we arrived. Martha grabbed Miracle and he and I went outside to talk. He started explaining that he did not know where we got off track and said that I was the best thing that had ever happened to him. He never wanted to be without me and Angel was lying on him. He promised he would never let anyone else come between us and asked if we could start over.

I looked up at him with my heart still guarded and said, "Yes, but on one condition. You need to check Angel if you want to be with me."

We went back inside for dinner and started laughing and enjoying time with his family. Monday morning when Hayden and I returned to work, he sent Angel an email and cc'd me on it. He explained to her that they were just friends and he didn't appreciate her trying to sabotage his relationship with me and how he could no longer counsel or be friends with her. When I saw the email, for the first time in my life I felt liberated and trusting enough to let go and fall in love.

We didn't date very long before he started to mention marriage. New Year's Eve, Hayden got down on one knee in the snow at his parents' house and asked me to marry him and I said yes! Martha was ecstatic when she heard the news, but she said it would be best if we didn't tell her husband right away. I didn't understand why at the time, and I just sort of blew it off. But it was funny that Martha, Yolita and I were planning the wedding and whispering whenever Pastor Tatum was around. It kind of reminded me of the movie, *The Color Purple* when Celie was sneaking around and learning how to read. Speaking of *The Color Purple*, Pastor Tatum had not taken his own wife to the movies since it reached the theatres in 1985. He wasn't the type of man that put a lot of emphasis on relationships, so why would he be excited about our engagement?

About two days later, Hayden called me all frantic on the phone asking where my wedding band was. I told him I had not been in his room and all I had was my engagement ring.

"What's wrong?" I asked.

"My parents' friends were here visiting from out of town and the constable is putting us out of our house; there are so many people going in and out and I think one of them stole it."

"Wait...hold up! Ya'll are being put out! Why?"

"I'll tell you later; but right now, I have to try and help my mom pack and look for your ring."

"Do you need some help?" I asked.

"Yes! These people are throwing our stuff out in the yard in trash bags."

"Okay, I'm on my way!"

All the way over there I was thinking, *how in the world could this be happening* and praying that everything was going to be okay for them. When I arrived, there was furniture and people everywhere... just like he described over the phone. I immediately started looking for Martha to check on her and see what I could do to help out. After all, she'd been so kind to my daughter and me. I finally found her sitting out in the detached two-car garage crying her eyes out. I put my arm around her and told her everything would be okay. She tried to pull it together, but I could tell she was in a state of shock. The real truth was Pastor Tatum was also a truck driver and he was on his way home from taking a load in his big truck and she did not know how she was going to explain everything to him.

Hayden had also just recently quit Optel to become a truck driver. He wanted to be a good provider for me and Miracle. I appreciated his tenacity to be a hard worker, but I had no idea how much the new job would keep us apart. Hayden ended up moving in with me and Miracle in my apartment. Yolita, Martha and Pastor Tatum moved into Martha's sister's apartment, while she stayed with their mother – Hayden's grandmother. Everything was very chaotic during that time and it was sad to watch as they tried to mend their lives back together.

Somehow, in the midst of all of the turmoil, we planned a pretty good sized wedding in a matter of about a month. Now mind you, Hayden and I had only been dating five months before we said "I do" on February 3, 2001. Martha had taken me to rent a wedding dress. We got married at Grandmomma San's church with Pastor Garrison presiding over our union. We were so tired afterwards that we went home and just crashed. We didn't open all of our wedding gifts until the next day while sitting on the floor in the living room like two big kids on Christmas morning. That was how he began to open up and tell me the truth about his family and the patterns of financial hardship that they'd suffered through many times before. He started by telling me how he and his parents were sitting on the couch in their living room a few weeks ago and a Constable came and knocked at their front door.

When his dad asked Martha what the man wanted, she quickly responded, "Oh, he said he was coming by to talk to Hayden about a job."

Hayden said he looked at his mother confused at the time, but he could see she was eyeing him to hush up, so he didn't say anything and just went along with the story she was telling his dad. Hayden later found out that the Constable was there to serve them with a subpoena to get out the house, but Martha did not want Pastor Tatum to know.

Hayden later asked his mom why she didn't just tell his Dad the truth. "What have you been doing with the money he gives you for bills?" he asked her; but she had no reply. Apparently, she was not paying the bills at all, but no one knows to this day what she could have possibly spent all of the money on. She was not a fashionista by far; so it couldn't have been on shopping or getting her hair and nails done. She was still rocking a Jerry Curl and mostly wore coveralls and old long dress suits.

Hayden said that she had done this many times before and that she had stolen his identity and opened up credit cards and phone lines in his and Yolita's names without their consent. He said Yolita is living with them because Martha had written thousands of dollars in hot checks in her daughter's name and wrecked her credit score to the max, so it was impossible for Yolita to get a place of her own.

Hayden went on for hours and hours divulging information about his past and how his dad would hit his mom and beat them all of the time for any little thing. By Pastor Tatum's own admission during his testimonies, I had heard him say before that he used to be an alcoholic and a womanizer; but I had no idea he was hitting Martha. I sat there in disbelief because for the past few months that I'd known them, they seemed like a nice, loving and perfectly normal family. Little did I know at the time what I had really gotten myself and Miracle involved in. Time would bring on a whirlwind of information and one tragic disappointment after another.

Hayden and I stayed in my apartment in Lake June Village for a few more months until the lease was done. He had started to complain about the neighborhood and developed an apparent paranoia for the residents. I tried to explain to him that paying $25 a month for rent was a blessing. Also, if we stayed and renewed our lease we would have an opportunity to save a significant amount of money to help get our life started, but he insisted that we move, so we did. We rented another apartment in Irving and ended up paying $950 a month. At that time, we had only been married about two months. It was around then that I'd went to the doctor and found out I was pregnant with our son, Christian. Hayden and I were very excited about the news. Our new place was close to his oldest sister Mariah, so we would visit them on most weekends.

Mariah, her husband James, and his daughter Jada eventually moved in with us to save money for the down payment on a house. This was not a good idea. I was pregnant, Mariah was stuck up, Hayden was always off at work and James was lazy. He was always cool, but just extremely lazy! I would wake up at 4:00 a.m. most mornings very uncomfortable as I got further along in my pregnancy. I tried to watch television to help myself go back to sleep and James spent about four nights every week out at the nightclubs, so one particular morning when I woke up, he was just coming home from the club. He was stumbling around because he had been drinking. When he went to the bathroom I could hear him peeing on my freshly mopped floor and then back into the water of the toilet. I was infuriated and disgusted! Something had to change and quickly. My one expectation was for them to at least help to keep the apartment clean.

It wasn't long after they moved in that I discovered that Miracle's brand new bedroom furniture had been destroyed by them sitting drinks and a leaking can of oil sheen on it. I was so huge, uncomfortable, irritated and mean. Speaking my mind has never been an issue for me! I was constantly asking them to keep the apartment clean and I was very mean about the furniture being damaged.

When I returned home from work one evening, Mariah was sitting on my couch with James who had just obviously been playing basketball and sweating profusely. *No home training, who sweats on someone else's furniture?*

In my frustration, I asked, "Mariah, have you seen Miracle's potty?"

"No, is it not in the bathroom anymore?"

"I'm sure it is, but apparently your husband needs to start using it because I'm tired of getting up every morning to mop his grown ass pee from my bathroom floor."

She looked at me very appalled and I walked away. Not long after that confrontation, Mariah and her family moved in with Martha and Pastor Tatum at their new home in Duncanville. I honestly did not mind them living with us at all. I was mostly bothered by the destruction of my furniture and their inability to clean up after themselves, but we were happy to have our apartment back to ourselves again. Mariah and her family lived with my in-laws for a few months until their new home was ready.

I took my wedding album to work one day shortly after they moved out, and this ghetto girl recognized James from the club. When I told her he was my brother-in-law she was shocked and said she could not believe he was married with the way he acts in the club. I never told Mariah what I was told, because the blood between us was already bad and still cooling off from when they moved out. But no matter how hard I tried to befriend her over the years, she shunned me so I didn't feel comfortable telling her about her husband's behavior anyway. Plus, she knew who he was married to before she married him.

On September 11, 2001, I was lying on the sofa when the breaking news on every station announced the attack on the twin towers in New York. I had never seen anything like that before in my life. It was so sad watching people fall to their death and others scrambling to safety. I was due to have Christian on October 10, 2001 which was also Pastor Tatum's birthday. Hayden took me to one of my weekly checkups for the baby with plans to go on the road right after the appointment. But once we arrived at Baylor Hospital, the nurse checked me and said she was going to induce labor that day. Hayden was upset because he wanted to go to work, but he called his dispatcher and cancelled the load.

The nurse made me walk around the hospital for hours to aid in opening my cervix. She checked me often and the walking was working…it made me dilate more each time I took a stroll around the hospital hallway. That evening, they put me in a room and punctured my amniotic sac to break my water and induce early labor. The pain was so severe that I requested an epidural and in a few hours my legs had swollen up and the lower half of my body went completely numb. The nurse saw my son's head and I didn't even know I was ready to push. On September 25, 2001, my handsome son – Christian Tatum – was born with gray eyes that later turned green then to hazel. He had curly hair and was born weighing my identical birth weight of six pounds and ten ounces.

Not long after Christian arrived home, Miracle realized she was no longer the only baby. She decided to pack up some of Christian's things and she drug them down the hall from her room. I asked her what she was doing and she asked us when we were going to take that baby back to the hospital. It was so funny that she was already territorial at only twenty-two month's old. She has always been naturally witty and hilarious. Hayden and I had also recently started the process of building a new home; so at the end of our lease, the four of us moved in with my in-laws to save money as well. We were so excited that we would go by where the new house was being built frequently to observe the building process. We saw the foundation and pipes being set up before they created the structure.

I was newly married, twenty-one with two small children, moving in with my in-laws, and all the while thinking we all got along pretty well for the most part. There were a few minor hiccups during the adjustment period, but I could have never imagined how bad things would actually become between us. Not long after we moved in, Hayden began acting as if he was regressing back to being a child. He had his mom wrapped around his finger. She would cook upon his request and cleaned up after him and Pastor Tatum continuously; leaving me feeling lost and out of place. But at the same time, I had never been taught how to cook, so I helped out with chores and spent a large amount of time reading to my babies and playing in their room or watching television. Martha was also very helpful with the children though, feeding them and helping with their baths. She's always been a wonderful grandparent to my children. I can never take that away from her and I will remain eternally grateful for her kindness toward them. She spends more time with them than any of their other grandparents and she spoils them rotten…even to this day. For that reason, I instill in them how much they should appreciate having a grandmother of her caliber. She loves and takes care of them just like Grandmomma Emily had taken care of me.

CHAPTER SIX

Married too soon & too young

At about 6:00 a.m. one morning, I overheard Hayden's parents in the kitchen saying that I needed not to be so jealous of Hayden's work schedule and needed to be more understanding of how hard he was working. I quietly backed away and returned to the bedroom with my children. Apparently, he had shared with his parents my concern for his imbalance between work, church obligations and our family time. I felt betrayed and outnumbered. I could tell their opinions of me were completely bias and not in the best interest of our marriage.

Come to find out, I was not so jealous and paranoid after all. Hayden had been frequenting strip clubs on a daily basis after work. He had become a regular customer; so much so, that he'd been spending the money for our bills and house savings on lap dances. After his discussion of me and our marriage to his parents, we argued even more than we did about the females he just couldn't seem to leave in his past.

He would always say, "I knew them long before I knew you," as if that was a justification for continuing relationships with other females.

We had gotten into an argument about his never being home one time and as he was preparing to leave, I followed him out to his truck. He was so involved with belittling me and trying to make me think I was just crazy and imagining things that he took a cup from his cup holder to pour out some water and a hot pink condom fell onto the ground. He was furious because he was busted. We did not use condoms. He jumped in the Ranger and sped away screaming obscenities and cursing at the top of his lungs. I was so furious that I followed him, ramming my car into his bumper and trying to make him stop and talk to me. Instead, he called my spiritual parents and mentors, Minister Jonathan and Cindy Black, and we talked to them on three-way. His sad explanation at the time was that because I'd recently had a baby and could not have sex for six weeks, he decided to ejaculate into the condom to keep the semen from hitting the ceiling of the truck and then he threw it in the cup and forgot it was there.

I lost it and screamed, "What fool do you think you're talking to?"

He was so embarrassed by his own obviously ridiculous lie that he hung up the phone, disconnecting our call. It wasn't until many years later that he half-confessed the real truth to that story.

Jonathan and Cindy Black had been introduced to me by Hayden and I became very close to them. We would lean on them for guidance, prayer and marital advice. They have always been there for me in good times and bad, and I am eternally grateful for our many years of friendship. Jonathan tried to tell me one day as he counseled me and Hayden about the condom incident that he thought Hayden had an anger problem. But I didn't pay attention to it at the time. I thought Hayden was just acting out punching walls and slamming doors because he did not want to hear the truth about how dead wrong he was in his behavior. The Blacks also referred us to counseling with the Pastor and First Lady of their church. We went a few times and then stopped because Pastor Harris and his wife were telling Hayden the truth about his behavior and setting boundaries between our marriage and his family. He became angry with the truth and refused to go back to counsel with them again. I had no desire to discuss our marriage with Martha and Pastor Tatum because I had quickly realized that they wanted to remain blind to any of my husband's faults. But even Pastor Tatum suggested that we counsel with a non-biased third party.

I also later realized that Martha was happy we had moved in with them so she could interfere in our marriage. One night in particular, Yolita was kind enough to take my micro braids down and Martha volunteered to help. Hayden was lying on his parents' living room floor watching television, and our children were on the adjacent couch with Pastor Tatum. Martha sat down behind me to "help" Yolita and I could literally feel her purposely ripping the hair from my scalp. I started crying, but I didn't know what else to do! I touched Hayden with my foot and he turned around and saw the tears streaming down my face. I mouthed to him what his mother was doing and why I was crying. He looked at me and shrugged his shoulders and turned back over to watch television. I was livid, hurt and confused.

When I shared the incident with Momma many years later, she said I should have just started screaming for Pastor Tatum or turned around and clocked Martha one good time. When asked about the incident in marriage counseling some time later with Pastor and Sister Harris, once again Hayden said he did not respond or defend me because he thought I was making it up. I think that statement hurt more than the actual act from Martha. He would say anything to protect his family and make me appear jealous and unstable. His mom treated me as if I was unwelcomed unless her husband was present. As a matter of fact, things got so tense with Hayden and me constantly at one another's throats that she told me I should just leave and let my husband and children stay with her. I did not realize at the time how she was speaking that into existence; all except for the part about leaving my children behind of course. The friendship Martha and I once had was obviously over. There were rare times when she and I could talk as two adults and share our experiences.

I had heard stories from Hayden and his sisters about their dad's temper and how he punished them severely when they were growing up, sometimes for no apparent reason. As a matter of fact, one night Charlotte, Yolita and I stayed up and they were reminiscing with me about their childhood till dawn. I sat there with them for hours listening and we enjoyed talking so much that none of us realized it was almost daybreak. But Martha had also shared with me that Pastor Tatum hit her on several occasions. In one instance, she said that they were sitting in a car and he was upset over something very trivial and he punched her so hard in her face that it broke her nose. She then shifted it to the side to demonstrate to me how after all these years it's still broken and crooked. She said she was afraid to get treated for it because she wanted to keep him from being arrested. She also told me that when she was pregnant with the twins, she'd followed him to another woman's house and overheard them having sex as she stepped up on the porch. But she was too afraid to confront him, so she just drove all the way back home and never told him she'd known where he had been that day. It was stories like those that made me get a clearer picture of the type of family they had and what I had gotten myself involved with.

In my own observation of Pastor Tatum, I believe on one hand that he truly does live what he preaches and he studies the Word of God fervently. But on the other hand, he would sometimes submit to his flesh and hit Martha occasionally in anger. I say this because over the years I'd seen bruises on her body and when asked how she got them, she replied from cooking. But to my knowledge, burns are not blue black; however, Martha's contusions were obviously caused by trauma that allowed blood to seep or hemorrhage into the surrounding tissue. Plus, the areas on her body where they were located would have meant she had to have laid down on the stove top to acquire them; and as skilled as she was as a cook, this was highly unlikely. She was often sad, depressed and in desperate need for attention. Pastor Tatum spent most of his time either working or at the church and even when he was home, he was always working out in the yard or gone to do some work on his big truck. As a result of being starved for affection and love, Martha had become so mentally ill that she poured a bottle of pills onto the floor and lie down next to them waiting for him to come home and discover her appearing to have overdosed. His annoyance at her antics was evident and he had no shame putting her on blast and telling everyone what she had done; unfortunately sometimes he even told her dirty business from the pulpit like when he discovered she had been stealing money from the church.

Hayden and I and the kids lived with his parents until our first house was finally complete. I had been working at Chase bank and giving Hayden my entire paycheck minus my tithes to help save for the $10,000 down payment for our new home. I also worked very diligently to clean up both of our credit scores by sending letters, paying off our debts and requesting payoff notices, etc. Our new home was a four-bedroom, two-bathroom house with two living areas and a huge backyard for our babies to have a swing set.

Signing all of the documents was an experience within itself, but we were so excited on our closing date that it was surreal. I remember thinking to myself, *now we can finally start our lives, raise our family, be happy and have some privacy*. Martha was not happy at all when the new house was complete. She called me into her room after hearing the news and said, "I hate you and I hate that you married my son."

I was speechless, but when she saw the expression of hurt on my face she said, "Don't tell Hayden what I said."

I promise if I could have seen her in the spiritual realm, her head was probably spinning around on her evil body. In addition to damaging my hair follicles, she changed the dynamics of our relationship from that day forward. That incident was just a preview of the many terrible exchanges she would have with me during the course of my marriage to her "precious" son.

I told Hayden what his mom had said after he saw me crying at the back of the church that Sunday when Pastor Tatum had just finished preaching. He came over and asked what was wrong and after I told him he confronted Martha. But of course, she claimed that she was just playing with me and she laughed it off.

With the excitement of buying our first home, things were great between Hayden and me for about the first three months or so. Martha would call literally five or six times a day in thirty-minute to one-hour increments. She would ask what we were doing as soon as I answered and it was so annoying I remember responding once, "The same thing we were doing thirty minutes ago."

If we told her we had plans, she would ask Hayden to come to do her a favor. Just random things like come find their dog Smokey because he had gotten off his chain. One day, the dryer caught on fire and instead of calling the fire department or Pastor Tatum, she called Hayden. She'd even show up at the door at times when we would tell her we were walking out to go see a movie or had plans. She was willing to do or say anything to keep us from going on with our plans for that day. Hayden was afraid to speak up for us, so that caused much stress and tension in our marriage. Martha was such a despicable monster-in-law that she would ask to go on a date with me and Hayden even though she knew Jonathan and Cindy were babysitting Christian and Miracle. *Now if we got a free moment from our children to go on a date, why on earth would you invite yourself to tag along?*

She apparently became so bored with her own life that she called Hayden one day claiming she didn't know where she was and she needed him to help her find her way back home. He found her in our church parking lot. You'd think after the last incident she would never pulled that stunt again, but she went missing overnight once before and slept at a hotel. I think she did it to try and teach Pastor Tatum a lesson about not valuing her as his spouse by not coming home. But anyway, we watched him pace the floor all night waiting for her to come home and she never showed up. I went to work that morning and Hayden and I were scheduled to go out for lunch together. When he was running late, I knew something was up! He called saying that Martha finally came home and she and Pastor Tatum had it out so bad that Martha was screaming for Hayden. He said when he ran to see why she was screaming, his dad had a gun to her head. He tried to calm Pastor Tatum down and talk him out of the situation, but he told Hayden this was none of his business and Hayden left promptly.

I was just disgusted at the constant drama that had become my life at that point and did everything I could to steer clear of his mother. I made it a point to only be around her long enough to say hi and bye. So that Sunday, she was annoyed with me for looking straight through her and she came up to me in church.

"I'm tired of you not talking to me," she said with much irritation in her voice.

"I'm just trying to give you some space," I replied nonchalantly, not wanting to engage her in any more drama.

As minister's and deacon's wives, we dressed in all white every first Sunday and had communion at the end of morning worship. As a congregation, we'd all go around one pew after another to shake hands. I would reach out to shake Martha's hand and she'd squeeze my fingers together so hard that my rings would cut into my skin and she'd pinch me with her thumb nail. She continued doing this until one Sunday I got tired of her actions and pinched her back; she never pinched me again after that.

With the exception of Martha's constant interference and need for attention, we were finally trying to act as a married couple should; at least from our young and inexperienced perspectives. We'd get up with the children often on our off days at 6:00 a.m. having praise and worship, studying the Bible and praying over our home and family. We would gather in the den to watch movies. Oddly enough, after we moved, Hayden would get home from work early, always beating me home when before he was constantly late. So he would cook dinner, straightened the entire house and give the children their baths before I arrived. I would cook some nights, but he was much better at it than I was. He had been taught by Martha. Sometimes he would also comb Miracle's hair so I wouldn't have to do it before daycare the next morning. Hayden would have a hot bath and candles surrounding our whirlpool tub waiting for me with my pajamas laid out and if I beat him home, I would do the same for him. On weekends, we would both clean the entire house together and do our laundry and ironing for the next week. Then we'd take the babies to the park or go visit with friends and family. I thought, *finally this marriage thing is not so bad at all and it can become pretty much what you make it out to be.* That was a correct assessment, but it only works when both parties involved are willing to be honest and diligent enough to pursue a loving marriage God's way.

Looking back, I realize that Satan was attacking our marriage on every end and we were too naïve to fight the huge spiritual battle ahead of us. The exciting feeling of moving into our new home was based on futile emotions that were only scratching at the surface of the real issues deeply embedded in our relationship. Our marriage was always a rollercoaster of emotions. Hayden had recently announced to the congregation that he accepted his calling to preach, and I was very proud of him; but things became much worse in our marriage. Women were like annoying flies, using the Bible as a reason to befriend him or to receive his individual attention.

We were frequently allowing ourselves to be led by emotions and that's so dangerous because feelings change often and therefore can be very unpredictable in times of anger. Little did I know, the other half of us had mentally checked out yet again! I guess Hayden had gotten bored with our playful banter and the peace in our home. I think part of him wanted to be a good husband, but the other part of him was still young and very much so single...at least in his mind anyway. He was so immature that he would shamelessly flirt with other women in my presence and he began to hide his phone at night. If he wasn't partici-pating in adultery as he proclaimed, he was dumb enough to purposely make it look like he was cheating on a consistent basis. He thought his behavior was cute. So of course, my insecurities were provoked and then I was labeled jealous and crazy for reacting to his many episodes of extramarital affairs or the appearance thereof throughout our entire marriage.

Therefore, in my own immaturity and allowing myself to be led by my emotions, I began to check his phone while he was asleep. Sure enough, there was some very inappropriate dialogue between him and a random female. Once I confronted him about it, he would lie and explain it away. But he got hip to me checking his phone, so he started deleting his entire call log and all of his texts; even the thousand and one calls and texts from his mom on a daily basis that he received before coming home from work. I was so hurt that when I did see a number in his car or clothes or any shady activity that just did not smell right, I would start yelling at him immediately by phone or in person.

One night, he went off the grid for hours and was unreachable by phone and not responding to any text messages that I sent. He finally came home really late claiming he got caught out on the road. He headed straight to the shower and he forgot to delete the call log and texts. There were several calls between him and a female he and I had already discussed and agreed he no longer needed to be in contact with because she obviously liked him a great deal. I could tell where they talked back and forth throughout the day and then no calls for like several hours until right before he got home. I'm no fool; it was clearly evident that they'd been together at some point. The worst part about all of it was that after I had forgiven him for cheating even emotionally with that person, he changed his cell number in an effort to work on our marriage. But apparently, he could not resist giving her the new number.

So when he got out of the shower, I confronted him about it. "She's just my friend and I don't have time to talk to you because I have to be in Lubbock by 7:00 a.m.," he said. He came flying in the door took a shower and flew right back out the door. It was about two o'clock in the morning. I didn't believe him so I followed him to the yard where he kept his big truck and his dad was there. He overheard us arguing and asked me to please go home because it was late and unsafe for the children and me to be out at that hour of the night. I complied and then my phone rang as I was driving off.

It was Martha. Apparently, Hayden had called her while driving to the truck yard to fill her in on our latest disagreement. *What grown man calls his mother to tell on his wife at 2:00 a.m. and what parent would listen and then have the nerve to impose at that hour?*

Martha was beyond angry and began reprimanding me for checking Hayden's phone. Out of respect for her as my elder even though I was a twenty-two-year-old adult, I told her I did not want to talk about it. Needless to say, we hung up and by the time the children and I arrived back home, Martha and Yolita were knocking at my front door at 3:00 a.m. Yolita and I were close; but it was apparent that Martha had hyped her up...escalating an already bad situation to a much worse situation.

I went to the door and asked, "What are y'all doing here?"

Martha replied, "My husband sent me over here to put you back in your place."

I was completely dumbfounded by her audacity. They came inside following me to the den. Martha was yelling at me and saying her son works too hard all the time to have to deal with me not trusting him, and that I should just leave him so that he could finally be happy. Yolita was not saying much until I began to retaliate and explain to Martha that Hayden and I were two married adults and we did not need her coming over at 3:00 a.m. to rectify our issues.

Understandably, Yolita wanted to defend her mom so she said,

"You not gone be disrespecting my momma."

To which I angrily replied, "Both of you are being disrespectful by coming to my home in the middle of the night tending to business that is none of your concern," and I asked them to leave.

I was so anxious and upset I accidently closed Martha's heels in the door before she could step over my threshold good. My phone rang and I thought *what now?* It was Pastor Tatum asking if we made it home safely.

"Yes, and your wife and daughter just left," I said.

"Why?" he asked."

"Martha said you told her to come by here to straighten me out."

"I don't know why she said that, I did not tell her to do that!"

"I know, thanks for checking on us though."

"No problem, I just didn't want y'all out this late. It's dangerous on these streets at night," and then he and I hung up.

I tried to get Hayden on the phone, but he didn't answer. I spent many nights like that; feeling alone in my marriage, crying myself to sleep and not knowing how to just make it work.

When Hayden finally got home from work the next evening, I was so out done from praying and crying out to God for my marriage. I had nothing left for him. So in an effort to keep the peace and also due to my lack of energy to endure yet another elaborate lie, I was silent for days on end and sleeping with Miracle in her room which drove him nuts. He got tired of me not talking and fussing with him about his stupid phone, so he decided to force me to talk to him. I thought he would be happy that I was starting not to care enough to check anymore. He was finally free to do whatever he was doing. I decided, after praying, that I could not change him nor make him love me like I loved him.

Because he lived just to antagonize me and drive me up the walls with anguish, he decided to charge into Miracle's room so hard that the door slammed into the stopper and pushed the imprint of the door knob into her wall. I was sitting on the bed reading a book. He started cursing and demanding that I acknowledge him, but I just kept looking at him and thinking, *oh Lord! Here we go again.*

When he saw that I was not going to respond to him spitting while he was yelling and screaming, he sat down at the foot of her bed and started apologizing. He said that everyone makes mistakes and she did not mean more to him than I did. He suggested changing his cell number again to prevent the squirrels and porch monkeys he had been committing adultery with from calling him anymore. He added that he was sorry for hurting me.

I had heard all of his lying and temporary apologies so many times before that it was like a broken record when he spoke and he'd just put a hole in the wall fifteen seconds earlier. I was tired of his women, his lies, his broken promises, apologies and all the other drama that he was bringing into me and my children's' lives. Usually, after he apologized, we would talk about it and I would just want to make peace, be done with it and move forward. But on that particular day and right after his bipolar moment of anger, I just wasn't feeling any of it. I just burst out laughing in his face. He was infuriated!

He snatched me out of Miracle's bed and knocked me to the floor. I was still laughing at him, but yet crying internally. I tried to run, but I only got as far as the hallway right outside her door. He straddled me and sat down on my abdomen; pinning my arms to my side and he started choking me with his huge hands. I was gasping and kicking violently. Of course I was thinking, *is this really supposed to help me forgive you?*

Still trying to force me to talk, he would release my neck momentarily and he kept yelling, "Oh, you gone talk to me or die today!" he was cursing and spitting.

My own stubbornness would not allow me to utter a word; plus, I was too busy trying to catch my breath. Then he took his fist and struck me in my head. I started crying and screaming for him to get off of me. He was way too heavy for me to force him off or flip him over, not to mention the fact that we were in the middle of the hallway floor so there was no room to even try.

"I'm so sorry, Nikki, I didn't mean to do that!" he shouted and he finally got up and stepped aside.

I didn't answer him. I just bolted for the master bathroom and locked myself inside. I could hear him screaming, punching the walls and breaking our things. He knew I had to leave soon to pick the children up from daycare, so he waited in the den area for me to come out. As soon as I came out with my purse and keys in tow, he grabbed me and pinned me to the wall; squeezing my arms so tight that my veins were turning colors. He was pleading for me to forget everything and just act as if nothing happened. He even asked what was for dinner.

"I don't know, but I have to go get the kids," I replied.

Hayden refused to let me leave and insisted on going with me. At first I told him I thought it would be best for me to go alone so things could cool off. But I realized he was not going to release me until I said yes. I agreed and I had to pretend that I had forgotten something in the bedroom. I waited a few moments and when I heard him getting something out of the refrigerator, I ran through the laundry room and into the garage. When I finally made it inside the car, he started beating dents into the top of my hood and he smashed my windshield with his bare hands. He was shouting for me to unlock the door.

I remember thinking, *this fool is really crazy*! I had to speed away from him and I could barely see out of the front window. Thankfully, the daycare was only two miles away. I picked up my babies and stayed gone for hours until I figured he had left for work and it was safe to take them home. We fought in their presence often and I always worried about how it was affecting them. Every time something like that would transpire, I would become distant and start to shut down for long periods of time, not realizing what was happening to me both mentally and physically. I was losing myself in our relationship. It was greatly affecting my interaction with people; but most importantly, it was affecting my interaction with my babies.

I was beginning to feel like, even though I was physically present in the lives of my children, I still missed out on an enormous amount of time enjoying their growth during those early years. I detested that so much because Christian and Miracle were all I had in the world. Their love for me was unconditional, and so was mine for them; yet, I was letting outside forces interfere with that. But I did not know how to get my thought life back on track.

Our fighting became a second language in our relationship. I too was guilty of vandalism. I had found more inappropriate text messages in Hayden's phone and got angry and thrown a brick into his truck windshield as he was trying to speed away to avoid addressing it. Drama and violence had just become the way we communicated, disrespected, and degraded one another on a regular basis. So much so, that often we'd sometimes forget what transpired to cause an argument to escalate to the point of us sleeping in separate rooms.

Pastor Tatum would often say, "Somebody gone get hurt or killed if y'all keep that up!"

I finally reached the point that I could not even stand to be in Hayden's presence. I would often pray over my attitude toward him before going home after work. I resented him for breaking my heart and for all the hurtful things he had said to me so much that it became a struggle for me to be kind to him when he was being nice. I remember praying and begging God to change the way I felt about him and for the way I treated him. Most of my prayers ended with me asking God to help me forgive Hayden and just move forward with our lives.

I soon realized that it was too hard for me to forgive him because he broke my heart so frequently and I could no longer trust him. A broken heart is very complicated to repair; especially when there has not been an opportunity for it to mend properly before it's broken again. But a broken spirit was causing me to lose myself completely.

Our church members, friends, and his family thought I was just becoming mean; but truly I was falling into a deep battle with depression. I'd experienced so much negativity in my life that I think I was becoming bitter and developing a dislike for all people in general... including myself. I had put up walls to protect myself and would rebel against authority because everyone I'd encountered in a position of authority had abused me in some way.

I now believe that is why I've had so many jobs that I can't even count them all. Let's just say it's well over twenty-five and I should probably be in "The Guinness Book of World Records." I felt so inadequate and unhappy that I didn't even know how to conduct myself in a professional setting. I had become a professional interviewee. The truth about my career is that moving from job to job was never because I didn't want to work. I knew exactly what to say to get a job, but my attitude and rebellion would not allow me to keep them for very long. That, along with the fact that Hayden would also call continuously and had even come to a few of my jobs acting a nut and gotten me fired. *As if I needed his help losing a job!* But I wasn't aware then that until I got out of my own way, the struggle would continue inside me until I passed the test and changed my attitude.

Hayden had become so immune to my heart aching for him to change. He just simply did not care! On one hand, I didn't know how to be a mother or a wife for that matter. But I was at a loss because I did not believe in divorce either, so I was stuck in an unhappy marriage. On the other hand, I had no clue how to continue living in a façade of a marriage and maintain a peaceful spirit or a healthy emotional balance.

Once the trust in our marriage was dissolved, it was downhill from there on out. I could no longer trust the one person who had promised to love me as Christ loved the church, and my walls were always up on indulging in infidelity myself. Over the years, men would pursue me in the grocery store, at the gas station and amazingly on the freeway once. Even several famous men that I'd had the privilege to cross paths with through work or an independent business opportunity had made advances toward me; from actors to NFL players.

But I would give them all the same response, "I'm married," if I responded at all.

One guy, who played for the Dallas Cowboys, saw Hayden and me together and he still had no shame in approaching me; but of course, I declined. In spite of what I knew my husband was doing, I never wanted to take it there on my own accord. Two wrongs do not make a right, and I loved him and I took my vows very seriously when I said them.

I just believed that if I kept praying for my husband and my marriage and trusting God, my life would finally balance out and turn around for good. I had to believe that to stay sane. But truthfully, I was living back in Hell at a different address and deteriorating slowly but surely once again. With Martha constantly interfering and our own marital pitfalls, life was about to blow in yet another huge storm.

CHAPTER SEVEN

Now what, Lord?

Hayden had tricked all of our money off in strip clubs, or buying stupid items like guns, baseball caps or fishing rods. Needless to say, we had fallen three months behind on our mortgage and exhausted every payment arrangement the bank could offer. Our mortgage at the time was $1,584, so there was absolutely no way we could catch it up. We received a foreclosure notice and a court hearing letter followed not far behind. The judge ordered us to be out of the house in thirty days. Hayden's first instinct was always to call his parents; they were his crutch anytime he would fall on his face as a man. The problem was that his training wheels never came off! I pleaded with him and tried to explain that as adults, we needed to just find a place of our own to rent, preferably further out. But he would not listen, so back to the storage our furniture went and off to Martha's house our family returned.

There was a thick cloud of tension looming between me and his family and yet, here we were moving back in to live with them. The children and I mostly stayed out of sight. I would go in their room to read to them or play games outside to keep them out of Hayden's parents' hair. I immediately became very diligent in searching for an apartment or townhome we could rent before the foreclosure hit our credit report and ruined it, which was very depressing considering I had worked so hard to clean it up. I'd visited quite a few places, but I remembered living in a townhouse with Momma when I was fifteen and I thought that would be nice and it would be big enough for the four of us. The first set of townhomes I visited, the owner said she refused to rent to people with children. I found that odd, but she had the right to utilize her property the way she saw fit. I kept driving around and I found a very nice townhome off of Danieldale and Highway 67. The owner had placed a sign in the yard. I took the number down, but of course I needed to speak with my husband before calling her.

When Hayden got in from work that evening, after we got the kids settled in, I tried to bring up the townhome in casual conversation. But he was extremely content living with his parents as an adult male with a wife and two small children; so he was not very receptive to any suggestions about moving so quickly. Finally, by that weekend, I was able to convince Hayden to at least drive by the property with me to check it out. Once we pulled into the driveway facing the garage, he said, "What's the point of driving by and only looking at the outside if we can look on the inside?" We called the owner's number and she agreed to meet us there. When she arrived, I could hardly wait for her to open the front door. There was a small porch and a cozy entry way. It had two bedrooms and one restroom upstairs; and another half bath downstairs along with the kitchen, living room and a small dining area.

After the quick tour, Hayden asked the owner how much the rent was per month. She informed us that it was $950 with a $1,200 deposit for individuals who needed second chance credit relief. By this time, we had already been back at his parents' house for several months, so we knew the foreclosure was already on our credit report. He then asked her if we could discuss it for a moment and the woman graciously stepped outside while we conversed.

I was elated that he was being inquisitive about a place of our own and I could see he was now interested in moving out; but our history together had shown me that trying to get the king of procrastination to follow through was like pulling teeth. So I did not want to get my hopes up too fast. But to my surprise, Hayden wanted to discuss moving in the following month to allow ourselves time to save the deposit and first month rent; I agreed. The owner was very understanding and kind enough to hold off renting it out to anyone else until we could come up with the money. She allowed us to complete the application in advance to get the process rolling.

I could not wait to move again. I hadn't completely unpacked when we moved to his parents' house because I did not want to get too comfortable in that situation. It didn't take me long at all to pack what little we did have unpacked. Martha was of course opposed to the news of our moving out. She tried to convince Hayden to just stay with them longer so that we could continue saving money. The gesture was nice, but it was always about ulterior motives for her and she was painfully obvious with her deceit.

It almost worked; Hayden started to back pedal on the townhome until I told him the kids and I were moving with or without him. Little did I know, we would be moving back in with Martha and Pastor Tatum in no time! The excitement of moving into a new space had always been a high for me. I enjoyed the unpacking and decorating a new place. Unfortunately, we were twenty-three and twenty-four at the time with two little children and raking in weekly daycare fees of $240 a month with no money management skills whatsoever. Even though we were married with children, we were still young and naive about adult life.

I was also singing in a local gospel group with Darrell and La-Tonja Blair as an outlet at the time. It really is a small world after all. They use to sing with Kirk Franklin and happened to be friends with Rodney from that era. Rodney claimed that he sang with Kirk Franklin...*anyway!* I enjoyed being around the group and feeling like I was finally a part of a family. But the gas driving to Ft. Worth and performances as far away as Frisco were becoming a tad too expensive for our budget, so I resigned from the group. Plus, unless Hayden cooked or barbequed, we ate out almost every night of the week because of my schedule, also making it difficult for us to keep up financially.

We would go to Hayden's cousin Nigel and his wife Tammy's house frequently; almost every weekend. If we weren't at their house, they were at ours. They were a couple around the same age as us at the time with three children of their own. Our families just enjoyed spending time together. Tammy was certainly a people person, so they would always have other people over for a barbeque and a variety of games. Tammy was always passing this horrific gas that just sat in midair like a thick cloud of smoke and I would make fun of her all the time about that. We all had really fun times together. We had gotten so close to them that if Hayden and I were not going to a family function, Nigel and Tammy weren't going either. We would spend so much time with them that they had become used to us arguing and yelling all the time. Going to their house was like a chance to get away for a weekend from all the constant bickering in our home, in public and even sometimes in church that we were doing. It was a break for me because Hayden was being entertained by Nigel; while Tammy, her younger sister Tonya and I were with the kids and hanging out amongst ourselves.

Hayden began to explain our financial difficulties to Nigel, and he in turn, introduced my husband to the term, *payday loan.* It was the devil in the form of a loan allowing you to rob Peter to pay Paul, so to speak. In exchange for your paycheck stub and bank account information, these businesses would loan you money in advance on a ridiculous amount of interest; and in turn, they basically retrieved your paycheck on your payday with interest. Hayden became very dependent on payday loans. So, inevitably we were behind on our bills; yet again, and agreed that payday loans were not a good idea. After a vicious cycle of these loans and it affecting our ability to make it payday to payday, Hayden said he would not get another loan because he finally realized that after the interest, he was paying back double for the loan.

One afternoon, our home phone rang and it was the payday loan sharks, but they asked to speak to Martha. I asked the lady on the other end of the phone how she got our phone number. She said Hayden came in and did a payday loan with Martha and provided our home phone number. I figured she must have mistaken Hayden for Pastor Tatum and gotten the numbers mixed up because they have the same name. So after taking the message, I hung up with her and called Pastor Tatum.

"Hi, Daddy," I said when he answered.

"Hi daughter, how are you?"

"I'm doing good; I was calling because the lady at the payday loan place just called here for you and Martha."

"Payday loan? I've never done a payday loan."

I could feel the veins starting to pulsate in my forehead. "Hayden must have gotten one for Martha, sorry for calling you at work, I'll talk to you later," and we said goodbye and hung up.

I immediately called Hayden. I could tell he was in his big truck because he asked me to hold as soon as he answered, so he could adjust the volume on his CB radio.

"Ok, hey baby," he said.

"Hey," I replied. "Uh, why did you go with your mom and do another payday loan?"

"Because I wanted to!" he snapped. I don't have to tell you every little detail of what I do."

"Well, that does not make sense when we are barely scraping by and living paycheck to paycheck ourselves. It's also not cool that you call yourself doing it behind my back."

"What did you do, go through my receipts?"

"No, the payday loan lady called asking for you and your mom, you idiot! I don't have to look through your dumb receipts because in all of your indiscretions, God always has a way of allowing them to come into the light."

He hung up the phone in my face and all I could do was pray and ask God to show him where he was wrong. I didn't want to call him back so that we would get into another argument, as usual, with us both taking turns yelling, cursing, screaming and hanging up on each other.

I was already upset with him for accepting a new job working with Sharita Folks, a girl who wasn't even classified as his ex. They just use to have casual sex together in college; and to make the situation ten times worse, she'd also just become a member at our church. Hayden told me, when we first met at one of his friend's weddings, that Sharita had slept around with several guys when they were in college. As if that's what I needed in my life...another girl at our church that my husband had slept with previously.

Martha was tickled to see me struggling in that area of my marriage. She seemed to get joy out of me being embarrassed. She taught our young adult Bible study one evening in Pastor Tatum's absence, and she told Sharita and the entire class about Hayden not being circumcised. Of course, Sharita and a few of his other exes were already aware of that, but as his wife, I was still embarrassed about Martha's admission because there were several of our peers also present. I did not understand why she felt the need to share that bit of personal information, other than the fact that she knew by doing so, it would embarrass me.

To add fuel to the fire of Sharita having a business relationship with Hayden, she would only agree to talk to him over the phone while he was away from home. It was something that bothered me, yet he allowed it. One day, she called and the phone speaker was so loud that I could hear her on the other end while he was standing next to me. As soon as he said he was at home, she asked what time should she call him back. He was on his way out the door, so he told her to call him in about fifteen minutes. I asked him if she was "just his boss" why he couldn't take her calls in my presence. As usual, he slammed the door in my face and burned off in his truck to avoid the confrontation.

Sharita started inviting Hayden, Miracle, Christian and I over for dinners with her husband and their two daughters. I was very reluctant to go, but curious enough about the mysterious phone calls not to indulge. I did not want to come off as unfriendly or anti-social and Hayden was the one barbequing at their home, so I felt it gave me a chance to see them interact with one another. He and Sharita would be in the backyard talking, and as soon as I walked out, she would always go inside until I came back inside again. During this ritual, her husband, VeShawn, was always in their garage. I was mostly left alone inside on their couch, even the children were in another room playing together.

Bottom line: my husband never wanted to set healthy boundaries in our marriage; therefore, it was a constant series of incidents involving random women that appeared evil and adulterous. He always rebelled against implementing anything I had learned in my weekly married women's group. He also was resistant to any advice we'd received through the marriage seminars that I had to drag him to or the counseling sessions we'd had over the course of our marriage. I never knew for sure if Sharita and Hayden were still having sex, but they both always made it look as if they were.

What I found out years later after she and her husband had divorced and both remarried, was that she had warned VeShawn not to talk to me. He said she was jealous of me because I was so beautiful and she felt threatened by my presence in their home. She was not the prettiest duck in the pond admittedly; so I understood her insecurity in that area after he mentioned it. Yet, she always invited us over and was practically throwing herself at my husband. I only indulged in trying to befriend her because we all went to the same church. Come to find out, she was a flirt everywhere we went. She started inviting me to girls' night out events and to the gym to work out and she would shamelessly flirt with all of the men present. This confirmed what Hayden had described to me as her "loose" college reputation.

Hayden was very popular in the church; especially with the female members. They would fall all over themselves to get his attention or a one-on-one consult to discuss personal issues or to get clarity on a scripture. His older cousin's ex-wife, Gomer Dabbs was the worst; she bent over in church one Sunday as we were walking out of service. Pretending to drop something on the floor, she put her rear end on Hayden's penis. Yolita saw her and said I should have taken my foot and kicked her over onto her head. He did not say a word to her, but he did apologize to me saying that he had no idea she was going to do that. Another lady joined the church after moving here from Chicago with her three daughters. I thought she was pretty cool at first that is until I realized she never really wanted to be my friend. She would also talk to Hayden and walk or drive away whenever I came around. What I came to realize by Hayden's own admission years later, is that he was telling everyone behind my back that I was mean and jealous. He took much pride in the fact that over the years, he had been falsely tarnishing my reputation to his coworkers, his family, our church members and friends for the sake of self-pity.

When he admitted that talking badly about me to others, whether we were getting along or not, made him feel good about himself and justified in his sins, it hurt me to my core. It hurt so badly because for all those years, I had been married to that man and hiding the reality of my life as his wife from the world. I was shielding him from ridicule while his betrayal and assassination of my character had become a script; one that he had repeated so often, he had committed it to memory. More people confirmed this deception on his part by saying similar things that I had heard before from others who Hayden had divulged them to. While he was defaming me, he also had comfort in the knowledge that he knew that I would always cover for him and not speak ill of him or his split personalities to anyone.

As a child I had always heard Momma say, "If it ain't one thang, it's another," and I was starting to learn exactly what she meant by that. We had not been in our quaint little townhome long before we realized there was an issue with the electricity. Our utility bill skyrocketed to $530 a month. We could not afford daycare, rent, gas, food and an astronomical light bill; it was just too much for us to handle monthly, so we ended up moving right back in with Martha and Pastor Tatum. I was more sad than mad. It just felt like my life had become this never-ending horrific roller coaster ride with no escape.

My life was consumed and revolved completely around Hayden and his family and friends. He never really wanted to visit with my family; so I was swept up into his entire world and surrounded by people who aided in enabling my husband not to grow as a man, let alone as a minister, husband, or a father. I felt trapped and suffocated because I did not have family that I could turn to and even if I had left him, where were my children and I going to live? So it was a double edged sword.

His family was always there to lend a helping hand in any way they could and that was admirable; but all of us living under one roof was not my cup of tea. Although Hayden enjoyed it immensely! It didn't seem to bother him one bit. I had always been a very independent individual; so as an adult, being dependent on other people was too much for me. That time, we stayed with his parents for about ten months… saving our money again. We did manage to save enough money to go on a Gospel cruise. It was our first trip, so after three years of marriage, we deemed the cruise with Darrell and Latonja Blair as our honeymoon. There were several other famous artists on the ship as well, such as Beverly Crawford, the group called Solo and so many more. We needed the getaway and managed to go out and tour the islands. We even rented a motor bike that I almost wrecked because it was too heavy. The one thing I will never forget about the trip was when we were walking through an outside corridor with a pool in the center, headed to rent the bike. Hayden knowing how extremely terrified I am of snakes, tried to call my name softly to warn me. He knew that I was so freaked out by them that I couldn't even watch them on television and I referred to them as s-word thangs. But before he could get his warning out to me good, I saw the red snake moving so fast from the sidewalk and all the way across the pool. I ran and jumped on the counter at the bike rental shop. We laughed about it for days. It made for a wonderful trip, but five days on a ship was way too long.

We were excited to get off the ship, but I was not excited to go home to Martha and all of her crazy antics of interference. We were not home long before she and I were upset with one another again. Miracle had disobeyed Hayden and he spanked her. But instead of Martha being mad at Hayden, she flipped it on me to avoid having to confront him. She heard Miracle in the other room crying and she burst through the door yelling.

"Nikki, I know you hear her crying and you sitting up in there watching TV."

"She's crying because Hayden just spanked her," I replied as she slammed the door. She went to check on Miracle and then came back in the room fussing at me again. Hayden was kneeling on the floor ironing his clothes and I asked her, "Why are you fussing at me; he's the one that popped her?" He just sat there, as usual, playing invisible. She gave me an evil look, raising her eyebrows and pointing her finger at me and I said, "Martha, I am not scared of you!"

Shocked at my response, she slammed the door again and I could hear her ranting and raving in the other room; but I ignored her. I asked Hayden why he just sat there and didn't say anything to his mother and he said, "She wasn't talking to me, she was talking to you." It was instances like that which made me feel like less of a person and more like an object in both Martha and my husband's eyes.

Martha would always interfere when we disciplined our children. She'd even lie for them at times to save them from a spanking. She was also upset because Hayden and I had recently contacted Rodney to meet Miracle and sign a letter that he and I typed up stating that he had chosen not to be a part of her life. Basically it stated that financially or in any other capacity, he was willing to sign his rights away as her father and give them completely over to Hayden. Surprisingly, by doing so, with that signed document, we would be allowed to have Hayden sign Miracle's birth certificate and get her last name changed to Tatum. At the last minute before the meeting, Hayden decided not to go with me, Miracle and Christian to meet Rodney at the park. Rodney's first time seeing Miracle before that meeting had been when she was four months old when he popped up at my apartment one day. Meeting him in the park was just his second time ever seeing her; she was four years old at the time and he didn't even know her name. It was very sad because she ran to him and hugged him as if she felt some sort of connection with him and then she asked him to push her on the swings, still not knowing who he was. He stayed for about twenty minutes and gladly signed the paper and I didn't see him again until Miracle was almost ten.

Martha was obviously still upset the next morning after the papers were signed. I was coming out of the bathroom and standing behind her, but she thought I was still in bed. She took the cordless phone and threw it into the bedroom door; I guess she did it in an attempt to scare me up out of my sleep. But I, in turn, scared her when I asked, "Why would you do that?"

She was startled and responded, "Oh, I dropped it by accident. I was bringing you the phone because I'm headed out for work."

I went in the room, crawled under the covers and laughed hysterically because she was such a habitual liar. I saw her with my own eyes throw the phone into the door. Hayden and I had already caught her listening at the door while we were having sex; twice. He saw her try to run when he opened the door. Now she had been busted throwing the phone at the door. The lady was as looney as any cartoon character I had ever encountered in my life.

With all of her antics on top of stealing my things while I was at work, breaking out my car window and running up long distances charges on my personal phone line, I was determined to get the hell out of that woman's house once and for all.

While driving around, I found a two-bedroom, two-bathroom apartment available for rent in Lancaster. I loved my husband and I was submissive, but this time I had to be proactive for fear that we'd been living with his parents so long that he would never want to move out again. I took some initiative and went to see the apartment alone. The manager offered me $150 off the first month rent during a look and lease on the same day promotion. I jumped on it! I paid the application fee and filled out the paperwork expeditiously. I called Hayden with excitement in my voice and surprisingly, he did not gripe at me. He asked if I liked it and how much the rent would be. I gave him the directions and he met me at the leasing office while the agent was processing our application.

The manager walked us back to the apartment so Hayden could take a look inside. It still needed the carpets cleaned and a fresh coat of paint; but once the application process was complete, she assured us that we would be able to move in, in two weeks. Hayden's only concern was the small master bedroom because we had a huge king-size bed in our storage. We moved in after signing a six-month lease because we still truly wanted to be in a house and would go driving often to look at available options in various newly-developed communities. We finally retrieved all of our furniture from the storage for the thousandth time and settled into our new place. I liked that our apartment was on the second floor, but he was not excited about having to carry all of our heavy furniture up the stairs. Sadly, whenever his friends or family needed help moving, they'd always ask to use our truck and he'd go help them move; but when we moved, it would pretty much be me and him doing all the work.

I remember Yolita coming over to help me unpack; she and I were always friends and I enjoyed her company. Miracle and Christian loved her tremendously as well and we were always happy to see her. Now that I think about it, she was the only friend I truly had at that time because all of my friends were busy with their own lives and drama. Yolita would show up anytime Hayden and I needed anything. The only thing about that was, since she was my sister-in-law, I never really confided in Yolita about the truths of my marriage or her brother's violent temper. We would mostly discuss the things we had in common such as movies or what was going on at our church. She, too, was private when it came to talking about her long-distance relationship to Percy. They had been dating since 1999, but he lived in Oklahoma, so they would take turns traveling to see one another as often as possible. But Percy revealed to me one day that he made mistakes in their relationship, while they were dating. I always knew something happened between the two of them because for as long as I had known Yolita, she was always on her phone with Percy. This explained why one-while when were all living at her parents' house, I noticed she hadn't mentioned him in weeks. I didn't pry or ask what happened between them and she never offered to talk about it. They obviously worked through whatever issues they were facing in their relationship because she ended up talking to him again and ultimately they got married. Yolita and Percy were dating nearly ten years before she finally presented him with an ultimatum for marriage. She had already purchased a new car and a new home when he finally moved to Dallas.

Percy is a very intelligent computer geek, but he was always fun to hang out with and very laid back. That was, until you beat him in a game of dominoes. He and Hayden would play dominoes nearly every time we all got together and they both would talk plenty of trash during the game; but if Percy lost, he'd actually pout. He was a very sore loser and his pouting just hyped Hayden up to antagonize him even more. It was amusing to see the two of them together; and we enjoyed spending time with Percy and Yolita when we had the chance.

The new apartment was starting to look and feel more like home. Martha would come by to visit, help us unpack and criticize of course. But, when she was not being snobbish, the kids and I would go shopping with her. She was alright to be around sometimes, but it wouldn't be long before she'd express a negative or judgmental comment toward me. I was learning how to treat her with a long handled spoon as my Grand Momma Emily taught me. Our apartment was not huge, but it was home for us and I was happy for us to be back on our own.

Hayden and I were still arguing frequently about his indiscretions, him being sneaky and his suspicious behavior. He still had no balance between home, church and his work life. So it was a constant struggle between us, but at least his parents were not in the middle of it refereeing in favor of team Hayden. I often felt like a married, single parent. I found a nice daycare called Kosmic Kids which was very close by and I was waiting for my training class at Compass Bank to start. I'd already developed a daily routine of getting up and dressing the children for daycare in the morning, and I would go into Miracle and Christian's room to read or play with them after giving them a nightly bath.

Life with two kids was interesting and they were witty and kept me laughing. I was very sad at times, but I needed to focus on my babies and myself; so I would go to the park to work out while they were in daycare. Hayden was very negative about my workout regimen and began to complain about my weight loss. But I stayed focused and tried to get him to eat healthy and participate with me. I thought this would be a nice thing for us to do together in an attempt to rekindle our friendship and our marriage. He did start for a while, and then he quit after two weeks of lean meats and salads.

I started noticing that after running, I felt extremely nauseated and I'd gag while brushing my teeth. I had lost about twenty pounds of weight by eating healthy and working out, when I found out that I was eight week's pregnant again. We hadn't planned for another child; but once I found out, I was hoping that a new baby would bring a positive change to our marriage.

When I was four month's pregnant, in an effort to build some rapport with my own family, I agreed to go to Vegas on a ladies' trip along with Grand Momma San, Momma, her sisters – Teresa and Kenya, and a host of other cousins, friends and various family members. I asked Tammy to come along with me out of fear of ending up somewhere in Nevada alone. Although I've always wanted to have healthy relationships with them, most of their mindsets are so negative. They still viewed me as the rebellious teenager they assumed I was; not knowing I was crying out for help, love and understanding from being molested at five, not to mention being raised by two selfish, irresponsible and mean parents.

Tammy had heard bits and pieces of the background of my not really being close to my family and she agreed to go with me on the trip for support. Hayden was not thrilled because he never wanted me around my family. He always said it was his way of protecting them from hurting me, but my thoughts were, *who's going to protect me from the hurt you cause in my life?*

After clearing the travel dates with my OBGYN, I was ready for a break and a change of scenery. Hayden was left home alone with the children for the first time in our marriage. He was finally going to get the chance to experience the daily responsibilities that I assumed for our children while he was out running the streets most of the time.

I would never advise anyone to fly during a pregnancy. There is something about the change in altitude that just does not agree with a developing, unborn baby. My stomach felt like my baby was trying to escape into my neck during the take-off and landing process. I was so miserably uncomfortable unlike anything I had experienced before.

Once the plane landed, Tammy and I were pretty isolated from the rest of the group. Momma's oldest sister Sharon was upset because we got on the shuttle bus right after the elderly people. As usual, she had to make a scene and cause the drama to escalate from one to ten in a matter of seconds. Tammy tried to explain to her that the flight had me feeling dizzy and I needed to sit down as quickly as possible, to which Sharon very rudely replied, "Well, she shouldn't have come pregnant if she wasn't going be feeling good."

I ignored her as usual; because anytime I encountered her, she had always seemed to be looking for an argument from me. That is until I finally got tired of it one day and lashed back at her while visiting Teresa who was in the hospital to deliver her oldest daughter. Ever since the moment that I gave Aunt Sharon exactly what she had been begging for, she's been nothing but civil toward me. The first lesson I learned in my college Psychology 101 class was, "You teach people how to treat you, by what you allow" and it is, in fact, a very true statement. I learned, over time, to also adopt that method when deal-ing with Martha and Hayden's family members that were rude to me.

Once the shuttle bus arrived at the New York, New York Hotel on the Vegas strip, Tammy and I grabbed our luggage and rushed off to the room. She was a little upset because I was too tired from the flight to go out that night. I just wanted to eat and chill for the rest of the evening and then start fresh in the morning. I decided to call home after I overheard Tammy speaking to Nigel from the bathroom. She went in there for a little privacy while on the phone, but I couldn't help but hear her conversation. She was informing him that we had landed safely and made it to the hotel. From her side of the conversation, I could hear that he was telling her that he and Hayden were out at a strip club. Tammy and Nigel had a pretty open relationship; I didn't realize just how absolutely open it was until many years later. Because of that status in their marriage, they were a little more lenient in some of the things that they did. They often visited the strip clubs together. But this was a boundary that Hayden and I established as a no-no at the very beginning of our marriage; it became a spoken rule in our marriage when he went to the strip club for his friend's party and didn't come home till the next morning. After that instance, strip clubs were off limits.

At first when I called him after learning where he was, I didn't get an answer; I tried back and Hayden finally answered, even though he was whispering.

"Why didn't you answer the phone?" I asked, fully aware of his reason why.

"The kids and I were asleep," he said.

Just lying!

"Baby, I forgot to tell you that the realtor called about a new house in High Pointe. It's in the third phase of the new subdivision and she wants to meet with us when you get back," he continued. Rambling as usual!

I was excited to hear the good news, but that was not my focus at that very moment or the purpose of my call. Hayden obviously did not have enough common sense to consider that I was with Tammy and that Nigel had just told her where they were. I immediately began yelling and screaming into the phone. Not only had he lied about his whereabouts, but he had also lied about the whereabouts of my children as well.

"I haven't been gone twenty-four hours and you are already up to no good. You said you were staying in to study for your sermon, Minister Tatum!" I shouted. "Where are my children?"

"They are at my mom's house, I just wanted to go out and have some fun like you're doing," he said.

"Figures, knowing Martha, she would support you and your shenanigans without a second thought."

"She didn't have anything to do with this; Nigel and I planned this outing the other day," I couldn't even hear a bit of remorse in his words.

"Well, that's funny 'cause you told me you had no plans and you wanted to put the kids to bed so you could hear from God and get your sermon down right for Sunday morning," I added with sarcasm dripping from each syllable.

"I am a grown ass man; you just enjoy Vegas and let me do me... bye!"

He hung up the phone in my face. What married man does that to a wife he supposedly loves? I tried calling him back several times; to no avail. He would not pick up.

After I hung up from my last attempt, Tammy asked, "Why would you throw the *Minister* card at him?"

Her words caught me off guard and caused me to second guess my actions; but only for a brief moment. "What do you mean *the Minister card*? Minister or not, Hayden is a man first," I said trying to emphasize the obvious.

"Nikki, sometimes women can be so mean and controlling toward their husbands that it drives them to cheat," her eyes seem to try and aid the point she was stating; but to no avail with me.

She, and no one else, had any idea what I had been dealing with for four and a half years of being married to a deceitful, disrespectful, verbally and physically abusive, belittling and snake of a preacher! I refrained from just breaking down and telling her the real history that Hayden and I shared. Truth be told, ironically speaking, with him being a Minister, I found myself always saving face and doing damage control for his image instead of being the better half in a blessed and ordained marriage that I deserved, but he was not equipped to deliver.

Instead, I replied, "I did not have to become mean for him to start cheating; but of course, once he started cheating, I became angry and could no longer believe anything that came out of his mouth. His tongue is that of a serpent snake. It's split down the middle. I encouraged him in his ministry because I believed in him as a Minister enough to know that in this gift from God, he is going to be elevated into becoming the man, husband and father he's destined to be. I had to believe this because otherwise, with so much consistent turmoil in our marriage, I would go bananas. I am Hayden's biggest cheerleader. So I always encourage him to sharpen that relationship with God in the hopes that once he begins to mature as a Christian, he'll then know how to love me back. I only see greatness in him when he's been spending quality time with God and when he's behind the pulpit. That's why I enjoy the rare times he prays with me and the children and when we still have devotion in our home because I know he can exegete the scriptures correctly and give an encouraging sermon. It's the life we live when he leaves the pulpit that frightens me; the moments when his words are put on the backburner to the flesh. The man and the Minister are two very separate personalities, like night and day. There is no Minister card that I am bashing him over the head with. I just make it a practice to always want to remind him of his responsibility to live the life he preaches and teaches our church youth about."

She was quiet as a mouse after that. We took our showers, ate dinner and fell asleep watching television.

The next morning, Tammy called Nigel and he told her that they had a great time and that all of the strippers at the club knew Hayden on a first name basis. Apparently he was a regular there. This upset me but it did not surprise me that he was still addicted to strip clubs. I still could not get Hayden on the phone because he was not answering my calls.

To take my mind off of the fact that my husband was making himself unavailable to me, Tammy and I went to breakfast and met the rest of the family for a tour on the strip. It was hotter than four pigs in a heating blanket in hell outside. Being pregnant with feet swollen the size of cantaloupes was not a pretty sight. We did an extreme amount of walking and I felt every bit of it in my legs and abdomen by the end of the day. We all went sightseeing, shopping and had lunch before catching a bus back to the hotel. We were so deep in number that we almost filled the whole city bus.

Kenya boarded the bus first and I was right behind her. I saw that she'd sat down and realized she was sitting next to a pretty peculiar looking homeless man with long dreads and she scooted over, only leaving about four inches of space for my pregnant behind to squeeze between the two of them. I tried to go backwards to find another seat, but there were too many people behind me to maneuver, so I had to squeeze my pregnant behind down in the seat. Kenya – who is always seeking approval and acceptance from Momma, my aunts, and Grand Momma San – insisted that I was looking for another seat because I thought I was too good to sit by the man.

"No, I said. "I'm dang near in his lap because it's so crowded in here."

Momma overheard us talking and asked what the problem was. Kenya said loudly, "Nikki thinks she's too good to sit next to that man."

Momma being as dramatic as Kenya said, "Nikki, you are not too good to sit there; he don't want you."

I tried explaining that I had absolutely no problem with sitting next to him, but it was a tight squeeze and that Kenya was sitting there first and had moved. I added the fact that she was the one that had snarled her nose at him and scooted over. This became a very loud and increasingly embarrassing exchange as Momma started explaining to all of the other nosey passengers on the bus her version of what she thought happened based on what Kenya said.

I finally got frustrated and lashed out at her saying, "It's not true and it's not worth causing a scene and escalating into a huge debate among twenty women and all these strangers on the bus."

I was fed up, hot, pregnant and most of all, tired of being misunderstood and accused of something I would never do. So in my tears, I leaned over and whispered to the poor man, "I am very sorry you had to listen to them humiliate you and me>"

He smiled at me and said, "It's ok."

I got off the bus at the next stop and walked all the way back to the hotel, leaving Tammy and everyone else behind. Understandably, Tammy was upset that I had left her, but we talked about it and I cried out and told her that I was just tired of reaching out to people who continue to bite my hand. I was tired of not being loved and accepted by my family for no apparent reason since birth. I added that I was so humiliated and hurt and that I was ready to end the trip early and go home.

Momma came to our room the next morning as if she took no responsibility in what transpired and she suggested that Kenya and I have a talk. I was thinking to myself that Kenya, Momma, Teresa, and I all needed to have a long overdue heart to heart.

I went to Kenya's room and she actually listened to me. I explained to her how the day before was a complete misunderstanding and that I was humiliated and extremely embarrassed. I finally got a chance to tell her that I can go months on end without seeing her and my family, and when I do show up, they are all snarling and looking bitter-beer faced, including her. I reminded her that I could call her sometimes when I had a parenting question, because she had been married longer than me and also had two daughters at the time, she would encourage me and pray with me over the phone. I told her how much I enjoyed and needed that support from her, but how once we got around all of our other family members, she'd act as if she was ashamed of me and didn't want them to know we talk from time to time. I stared her dead in the eyes and told her that it made me feel like she didn't want to be kind to me in their presence for fear of what they would think of her. It seemed to me that she would always go along to get along, and that Teresa was always monkey see monkey do behind Kenya, so my relationship with all of them was a never-ending vicious cycle.

Kenya said that she did not realize she was treating me that way and we both cried, hugged and made up. But our relationship is still not one that any sisters should ever experience. She's no longer mean when I see her. She and Teresa are very close; they hang out together often, and one day they ran into my friend Diana at the Texas State Fair. She asked why I wasn't with them and they replied, "We don't fool with her!" She said they thought it was funny, but she was puzzled and upset. Also, Kenya called me to invite me to go with them to take Momma to the nail shop and out to lunch for Mother's Day. I was so excited and thinking my prayers had finally been answered that I took off of work for that day. I was happy, thinking that the outing could be a start to me having my own outlet away from Hayden and his family for a change.

The morning of the outing, I called Kenya to ask what time we were meeting up, and she said, "Oh! Me, Teresa and Momma went yesterday."

I was so hurt and disappointed. How is it that three people can be raised together by the same person and become total strangers as adults? I wished Momma, Teresa, Kenya and I could talk things out someday and maybe they would even take into consideration my feelings and perspective. But it saddens me to know that if I died today I wouldn't know if my own sisters loved or cared for me. I just believe God is still working on the three of us as a family unit. However when I watch shows like *Tia and Tamera* on E! and *The Braxton Family Values* on *WE* TV. In those shows it was hard not only to see how close knit their families were, but how loving, supportive and understanding Mommy Evelyn is toward her daughters in the show. I may be a little too old for her to adopt me as her sixth daughter, but someday I hope to spend time with her and the Braxton sisters teaching me how to instill the same special bond that they have into my children. Any movie with sisters bonding and hanging out or a close mother-daughter relationship brings tears to my eyes. Kenya and I were in desperate need of much more than just a few moments alone in Las Vegas to talk things out and establish a real bond and friendship.

What I concluded later was that Kenya and Teresa have no desire to be close to me because of the lack of my relationship with Momma, which I cannot control. I had spent years trying to create a friendship with her as well. I was fresh out of ideas. So once I gave my entire family to the Lord in prayer, my burden of acceptance from them was lifted. When I see them, I'm cordial and I still invite them to my kids' parties, etc. I kill them with kindness and I don't mention the obvious elephant in the room because they would love to just write me off as crazy for bringing it up. Unfortunately, the downfall is I only learn what's going on with my sisters and my nieces via Facebook. They never reach out to me. But I'm still trusting God to fix it! I don't know what made me think going on a vacation with my family was a good idea though.

On the last day of our trip in Vegas, all of the women went to breakfast together. I saw Auntie Nachelle in the lobby and tried to speak to her. I kept repeating, "Good morning," but I didn't get a response from her. I thought she didn't see me at first because there were so many people in the lobby, so I started waving. But as I got closer to her, I realized she was ignoring me on purpose. She treated me as if I was a common stranger. I guess she was still mad about the incident on the bus, but who really knows...she could be childish and hateful at times too!

I just brushed her off and shuffled my pregnant behind to the restaurant for breakfast. We had only been seated about five minutes when the next idiot of the bunch decided to try me. Being her usually rude and obnoxious self, my Aunt Sharon started talking badly about my Grand Momma Emily, saying how she smiles and laughs too much. *You have to be miserable in your own life for the laughter of an elderly woman to be a problem for you.* She hardly ever saw my granny. I think she just wanted to get underneath my skin. Of course I spoke up and came to her defense in her absence. As far as I was concerned, she was the only real grandmother I had anyway. "My grandmother is not present and you are not going to sit here and ridicule her for being cheerful." I said. She looked at me and rolled her eyes, but well aware that she was about to get embarrassed if she kept it up. This was the cherry on top of the trip for me. I was beyond ready to return to DFW

Airport and get home.

As we began the flight home, I became nauseous on the plane. I tried to ask Auntie Nachelle for help because she was sitting on the row in front of us and everyone else was asleep. She rolled her eyes and turned back around as if I hadn't even spoken to her. Thankfully for me, the flight attendant came by at that moment and gave me a paper bag. I just don't get my family. They can be such bullies at times and then wonder why I rarely come around! It's hilarious!

Once I finally arrived home, I realized I still had to deal with Hayden's strip club fiasco. He asked me about my trip and rolling my eyes I said, "I'd rather talk about you first!" I asked him about being a "regular" at the strip club. He confessed to being addicted to strip clubs and that he had been spending our bill and grocery money on private rooms and lap dances for years. He said he started going almost every day after work. In my mind I thought, *no wonder you are never home with us.*

I was so upset and still sick from the plane ride that I didn't even respond to him. I just went and took a shower and then cried myself to sleep. When Hayden came to bed he woke me up to apologize and I was silent. I did not want the evening to turn into a 2:00 a.m. Jerry Springer segment. He then asked about my trip to Vegas again. When I told him all that had transpired, he replied as usual, "Your family does not need a reason to be hateful towards you! I am convinced that it's because you look better than all of them put together! They dislike that you're pretty; so therefore, they try to justify mistreating you." Your family has made it very evident that they have no concern for you and don't care about your feelings. They have made up in their minds that no matter how nice you are to them that they hate you and there is no relationship.

"I disagree. I've never thought that," I said. "I still think it's because they dislike my Daddy."

He hugged me and I laid back down. What's so funny to me is my family treats Hayden like royalty simply because he's a Minister; but they treated me like a criminal. All the while, they never knew that he really did not care for any of them at all. He always said they were too negative, loud, and that they were always gossiping. But he was a master at being inauthentic with people and a terrible Messy Marvin himself. There's nothing more unattractive than a man who gossips more than a woman.

I was hard pressed with a million thoughts running through my mind that night, so it was very difficult for me to fall asleep again, but Hayden dozed off in no time. We have been struggling financially for years and I had no idea this fool was giving those squirrels our money. Then I thought to myself, *I give him the tithes from my check, surely he could not be that idiotic. But Martha was stealing from the church once upon a time and they say the apple doesn't fall far from the tree. Who knows? Only God!*

Thankfully, my relationship with the Lord was very strong at that time in my life. If not, I don't know what I would've done. My mind was racing and I couldn't sleep. To make matters worse, we had rowdy neighbors who would come to sit on the green box underneath our bedroom window at 3:00 a.m., talking loud and sometimes arguing.

No matter how many times we'd called the police or the security guy in our apartments, they always returned and that night was no exception. I was so ready to move! I'm a light sleeper, so I stayed up all night, lying in bed praying.

I went to work the next morning completely exhausted. I felt a sharp, horrible pain with every step I took, so my doctor asked me to come in just to check things out. He said the pain I had was being caused by the baby resting on my sciatic nerve. He ordered me to bed rest for the rest of my pregnancy. I'd only been working as a personal banker for a few months, so I lost my job and unfortunately, I did not qualify for a short-term leave. I was pregnant, stressed, bedridden, and considering separation or divorce for the first time. We had been to numerous counselors and it never seemed to help us much because we were not consistent in implementing the tools they'd provided to salvage our marriage. Even with the newest attack on our marriage, I knew that Hayden's apology only meant one thing when he said it and that was, *let's just ignore the stripper issue and move forward.* In other words, stop talking about it.

CHAPTER EIGHT

Lead Me Father...please hear my cry

I could not wait to meet my baby girl, but I was so bored on bed rest; all I could do was watch movies and TV shows. I watched *Woman Thou Art Loosed* for the first time and the movie vastly penetrated my spirit. God used it to inspire me to write this book and unleash some of the pain I had been holding on to for years.

God began to pour out the words to me daily. I could be asleep in bed, and as the words began to flood in, I would have to grab a paper towel or anything I could find to write down what He was saying so I would not forget them when I woke up. I've never felt so on task and purposeful in my life before I began to write out of obedience. I was very excited about God using me as a vessel and thrilled to experience what He was bringing forth in such an amazing endeavor. Writing this book gave me a release and brought healing into so many different areas of my life. Putting my story on paper was liberating and I could not wait to see what God had in store for this plan. I started spending hours on end typing and writing rough drafts in an old notebook. Hayden thought it was a good idea and was very supportive of my efforts to become a successful writer. Martha expressed that she thought it was just a waste of time, but I could not allow her to discourage me and all I had was time on my hands. Since I was on bed rest, I could only go as far as the restroom before I was supposed to sit down again.

When Hayden got in from work one evening, he said that he had spoken with the loan officer for the house we applied for. Against my doctor's wishes, I went with him to meet her at her office. She had gotten an approval for us to move into another brand new home. We were ecstatic and God was right on time with that blessing because our six-month lease was just about up. Plus, we were happy to be leaving our noisy neighbors and the 1,500 ants that frequented our apartment on a regular basis, lining up inside on our back door whenever it rained.

Christian and Miracle helped me pack up their toys, and Yolita and Martha helped to pack everything else. We were finally getting into another home after being denied over and over due to the foreclosure in 2002. The new house is 2,784 square feet, two stories with two and a half bathrooms, four bedrooms, a game room, a huge backyard, two living areas and two dining areas. *Ain't God good! He did that!* It was about four miles from Hayden's parents' house, but we were on cloud nine and very thankful to get it. There was plenty of room for us and our two – soon to be three – children.

Not long after we got settled in, Hayden bought a second big truck and hired a guy from our church to drive it. He had recently bought himself a new Chrysler 300 and a Chrysler Pacifica for me. I asked him if he thought we were getting in over our heads again. He said no, and that I needed a new car because the fuel pump on my Alero was shot and that he deserved a new car because he'd had that old Ford Ranger since high school.

"I work too hard not to treat myself," he said. "2005 is just our year; we were in the valley, now it's our season to shine baby."

"Well, I just don't want us to lose this house too, because I am never going to live with your momma again and I mean that!"

He said not to worry and brushed me off. He was leaving for work and I'd been having what I thought were small Braxton Hicks contractions all that day. He kept asking if I was ok and did I think I was going into labor and did he need to stay home from work that night. I told him I was fine and I began walking around the house, cleaning and keeping busy. He left for work and Christian, Miracle and I fell asleep downstairs playing games and watching the movie, *Finding Nemo*. I took each of them upstairs to their beds and then crawled in our bed and fell off to sleep again.

At about 2:00 a.m., I was abruptly awakened by an excruciating pain that hit me like a two-ton bulldozer. I tried to just lie back down, but quickly realized I was in labor instead of just having Braxton Hicks contraction. The pain I was feeling meant business! I did not want to panic or wake the children, so I called Hayden. He was too far out on the road to get back home to me, but he called his Momma. Martha and Pastor Tatum rushed over to our house so fast that Pastor Tatum said Martha was about to run out the door with one boot on.

She stayed with the children and Pastor Tatum rushed me to the hospital in my car. My contractions were about five minutes apart and I was screaming my head off and keeping him posted on the time.

You could tell he was afraid, because I'd never seen him speak with panic in his voice. But he was determined to help me and he got me over to Charlton Methodist as quickly as possible. He was driving my little SUV on three wheels and it was hilarious, in hind sight, because he kept saying, "Hold on, we're almost there, just hold on!" Once we arrived, the triage nurses quickly rushed me to a room and I stepped into a gown and climbed into a hospital bed. I was still screaming bloody murder when I overheard one of my nurses ask Pastor Tatum if he wanted to come in the room. He promptly replied, "No, her mother is on her way, my son just called her." We still laugh about that night to this day!

When Momma and Auntie Nachelle arrived, my doctor still had not made it and I was screaming the name of Jesus by then. Auntie Nachelle came into my delivery room and Momma took off running down the hall when she heard me screaming. I was begging for assistance and because I could feel her head approaching rapidly, I was afraid that my baby was going to tear me if the doctor didn't hurry. Auntie Nachelle reassured me that everything was ok and that the baby was not going to tear me. The nurse was prepping the newborn bed and I was in so much pain I was up on my feet in the bed.

After an hour and a half of labor, I let out one more scream and simultaneously, out popped my baby girl and in walked Hayden and the doctor. She landed at the foot of the bed and I was amazed that God and I had just delivered the baby ourselves.

We moved into our new home October 27, 2005 and on December 10, 2005, I gave birth to a beautiful baby girl with a head full of coal black hair. Braylin was six pounds and seven ounces in weight when she was born and she looked just like a baby doll. With her birth, as well as the birth of our other children, Hayden was present to cut the umbilical cord and he stayed at the hospital with me overnight after I delivered our first two children. He was very attentive and would bathe me and make sure I was good.

Braylin was a very good baby; she only cried when she was hungry or wet. The next day, I was learning to breast feed her when I heard a knock at the door. I said, "One second, please!" but Daddy and his new thirty-two-year-old girlfriend, Carissa, just rudely walked into my room anyway. He was fifteen years her senior. *Gross!* I was exposed and frustrated so I tried to hurry and throw a blanket over Braylin as she nursed.

Daddy said, "Ain't no one second, I'm yo Daddy! You ain't got nothing I ain't seen before."

I was trying to ignore him to avoid confrontation, when I noticed Braylin was very still and extremely quiet to be nursing so I moved the blanket to peep at her. She was turning blue! My huge, engorged breast was covering her little nose. I panicked and became upset as she was gasping for air. *Guess I was not a breast feeding pro just yet!* Tammy came in soon after to visit also so she called the nurse in to check the baby out for my comfort. I was so happy when Daddy, and his new flavor of the week that he frequently picked up from the city bus, left my hospital room. He never has anything positive to say and it's painful to be in his presence. All he ever talked about was Momma and when they were married in 1981 and how she had him paying child support for me, and how his other kids' mommas had not put him on child support. I got so tired of hearing that over and over. He was like a broken record. He would suck the energy from any room like a blood-thirsty leech; but he would always complain about how me and my siblings never stopped by to see him. I didn't want to go sit and visit someone who bashed me for leaving college as if he has a degree. Nor do I want to spend time with someone who tells me repeatedly how my being born was a mistake and how much my being born ruined his life. I had heard it a thousand times; and quite frankly, it was hurtful enough but had become beyond annoying. Thankfully, Braylin and I were released from the hospital the next day. I could finally care for my baby with some privacy.

Miracle and Christian had been at Martha's house while I was in the hospital. I was very happy to see them and they seemed to be excited about their new little sister. Even at the ages of four and six, they were very protective of Braylin and did not appreciate many people holding her at all. I stayed at Martha's for about a week to recuperate and she helped me with the children. But after a week, I was happy to go back home and continue to learn more about how to reduce the pain during breast feeding. I had to brace myself before Braylin latched on. It was painful, but I had heard that it was very beneficial for her body and would also help flatten my stomach. I just wished I had known that when Miracle and Christian were newborns. I had gained so much weight it was ridiculous. I loved to run and workout, but my eating habits were deadly so it defeated the purpose.

Braylin and I missed the annual Christmas celebration at Rocky Springs Baptist Church because she was only two weeks old and I did not want to take her out so soon around that many people, especially during the cold and flu season; so we stayed in until mid-February just bonding and chilling at home. Still high on the happiness of a new baby and a new home, I made an attempt to reconnect with my husband and suggested we take a road trip. Alvin Jr. suggested I call resorts and hotels to sign up for a ninety-minute presentation and in return for listening to the presentation, I would receive a free night in a suite. I was all for saving money whenever possible, so I signed up to hear the vacation pitch at the Sunbay Resort in Arkansas and Hayden and I got a two-bedroom suite with a Jacuzzi for next to nothing.

We drove there and stayed a few days while Cindy and Jonathan kept our children. We almost bought the vacation package after the sales pitch, but decided not to. We visited the bath houses and got massages, but before we could enjoy a hot bath I had to go buy another breast pump. My breasts were too engorged and painful to relax. We enjoyed our time away and I don't think we argued once the whole trip. That trip was the calm before the storm.

As soon as we arrived home, the chaos of our everyday life did not take long to resume. Reality was back! We were at church hanging out after morning worship as we often did. Every week either Hayden would barbecue or cook, we would eat dinner at Martha's on Sundays or we'd all go out to eat. But we had to wait for Pastor Tatum to finish up at church first. While sitting in the sanctuary, I was telling everyone about the resort and Yolita asked me if she could see the pictures from our trip. When I went to Hayden's car to get them, he had two different females' phone numbers in the car and $300 hidden in the arm rest. I was livid and immediately went searching for him. He had just finished preaching and was in the back building doing only God knows what. We only used that building if dinner was being served at the church or for special occasions like Braylin's baby shower.

I passed him the two scraps of paper and asked who they were and he swore I had not found the numbers in his car. He accused me of trying to set him up to tell on himself. I asked why would I write down two random numbers and put them in his car then bring them to him; that made absolutely no sense. He was always trying to flip any issue in our marriage to deflect the negativity off of him. He was never man enough to tell the truth and own up to his mess.

We ended up getting into a heated argument with no regard to the few members that were still present at the time. We ended up taking the children and leaving his family behind. We argued all the way down the freeway and he became so angry that he took my head and slammed it into the passenger side window; holding me there by my neck while driving all the way down Clark Road. The children were screaming and I could not make him let me go. He drove into Albertson's parking lot and got out of the car and started yelling and beating on the hood; denting it. I was a mess emotionally and physically. My eyes were bloodshot red, my hair was mangled, and I could not stop crying.

We all got out of the car and Hayden and I continued arguing at the front of the store. I walked away from him, as usual, to avoid being further embarrassed in public. He never liked for me to give him the silent treatment or to walk away from him while he was angry. He liked the attention from onlookers. So while I was holding Braylin and pushing Christian and Miracle in the grocery basket, Hayden ran over and grabbed me by my neck and started choking me in the store. He hit Braylin in the head trying to get to me and she was screaming to the top of her lungs. I started screaming for help and he let me go. I was so distraught that I left the few groceries I had managed to put in the basket, took my children, and got back in the car as fast as I possibly could. The children were terrified and so was I. I knew once we made it home things would get ten times worse. This same man had just finished preaching a phenomenal sermon, taught Sunday school and led the praise and worship team; but on any given day, he could turn into a ferocious monster.

I never understood how he felt entitled to be so violently angry and yet he was the reason for distrust in our marriage. He was the one that was always doing stupid things and getting caught. It was as if he wanted to be caught and in his own immaturity, he would brag at times about his indiscretions. He got pleasure in watching me cry and wilt in agony over him. He'd even mock me crying sometimes and laugh about it like a two year old.

After yet another horrific night in the Tatum household, I got up early the next morning and went to get certified to open an in-home daycare to generate some income. By doing so, I could save $1,200 a month on daycare and could stay home with my own children. It was not a full four months of me being a daycare provider when I realized that having my own newborn, my two young school aged children along with watching a six-week-old baby boy, a little girl in first grade, and three bad brothers ages: eight, six and two, was way too much of a load for me to handle at that time.

I don't know if I was suffering for postpartum depression or if it was just the weight of my so-called marriage pulling me down. Hayden was also complaining about the children still being there when he got in from work some evenings. Once I reminded him of the late fees for delayed pick-ups, the weekly tuition we were receiving per child, and the food program money we were receiving, he stopped complaining and started helping with the daycare responsibilities.

But nevertheless, I closed the daycare and was referred by one of our church members, Lanitra Garrison, for a job at Plains Capital Bank way out in Plano. It was over an hour there and back with traffic, which I hated; but I enjoyed being a teller again. Lanitra is the wife of Everett Garrison; he and I grew up together and attended his grandfather's church during our childhood. I referred him to our church to become the new choir director and his wife and I became very close. Our friendship is what made her help me out with job leads.

Our marriage had become like a semi-dormant volcano that had been boiling at dangerous temperatures for years. It had almost become hot enough to explode and escape into the air, while destroying everything and everyone in its path without remorse. I hated the woman I had become. I was mean, bitter and unhappy. Hayden was starting to be gone more and more, and the kids and I were very accustomed to his frequent absence in our home. Lanitra was one of my closet friends and we enjoyed being in the church choir together. She's the only woman I had felt open enough to express the deeper truths of my marriage to, and she seemed very compassionate and concerned about my wellbeing.

I had only been working at Plains Capital for about a week or two when I realized that I was experiencing the same gagging reflux while brushing my teeth that I previously had when I learned of my pregnancy with both Christian and Braylin. My baby girl was only six months old at the time, but there was only one way to find out. During our lunch break, Lanitra and I decided to go purchase a pregnancy test and while sitting inside of a Taco Bell in Plano, I took the test in the restroom and we waited for my results. Sure enough, the test read positive and I was completely floored. Hayden and I were rarely having sex at the time and yet I was pregnant again.

I was still indulging in pornography occasionally to satisfy my own needs since I wasn't getting sex from Hayden on a regular basis. I had even deceived myself before and tried masturbating without watching pornography or I would think to myself, *well, I'll just look at the pictures and not push play. Because the sin was in watching those movies not in masturbating, right?* That's the lie I would feed myself while satisfying my sexual needs alone. Masturbation is defined as self-abuse. In the years of struggling with this sexual affliction, I've probably thrown thousands of dollars into the garbage. I would buy one movie, watch a section of it once or twice, get convicted by the Holy Spirit, and then throw it out. Then I would wait about six months to a year or longer, and then fall for the same temptation again. That was the cycle of my sexual addiction.

But you can't play with fire and expect not to eventually get burned. Just like any other bad habit, you have to take life one day at a time in order to change. Hayden had not long ago asked for a fast from sex with me, so I am sure he was still watching pornography in his big truck too. He said the physical fasting was mentioned in the Bible and could help us get our marriage back on track. Of course I did not believe him, and I knew he had to be up to something; but with him driving so far away for work, there was no way I could ever see it with my own eyes.

After taking the pregnancy test, I came home from work later that evening and Hayden was between job assignments at the time; there were no workloads for him, so he was home with the babies. When I walked in from the garage, he was lying on the couch and the children were watching television. I pulled the pregnancy test from my purse and handed it to him and to my amazement he shouted, "Whoo hooo!"

I was puzzled because my sentiments were so opposite. Then reality hit him and he thought about how sparse the trucking industry was at the time and his demeanor changed. He was in deep thought! I too was very shaken up. I felt blessed for the blessing of having another child, but amazed by the fact that they would be so close in age. *Only fourteen months apart! Wow.* The reality of that sunk in real fast.

When I woke up the next morning at 5:00 a.m. to head to work, it was very cold and pouring down raining outside. I got as far as New Clark Road and made a U-turn. I was so taken back by the fact that I was pregnant again, that I was just going to return home and quit my new job because my mind was racing, not to mention the fact that I was not up to the long commute anymore.

While turning around, I heard the voice of God say to go back. In obedience, I turned the car around and picked up a young mother with her two children. I had noticed her hitchhiking when I first passed her, but was reluctant to stop. Picking up strangers isn't a safe thing to do, but God told me to give her a ride, so I did. She put her two year old in Braylin's car seat, and was hiding a newborn under her soaked jacket. I asked where I could take her and she said to the Westmoreland train station. She was trying to go enroll in a trade school. When I heard where she was going and what she was doing, I encouraged her to see it through to the end. She was several years younger than me and I explained the many times I'd tried to go back to school but had failed to complete it. She was determined to get to the school and was walking in the rain with her children to try and make a new start for herself. I was glad I went back for them. The woman expressed how grateful she was for the ride, and then I went home.

As I drove home, I was riddled with confusion and pondering how I was going to make it in life with an absent husband, a terrible marriage and four children. I knew God was going to keep me; I was just trying to wrap my head around it all. Lanitra was very disappointed when she learned I had quit my job, but she also understood where I was coming from.

During the pregnancy, there was so much going on in our lives. My doctor placed me on bed rest as a precaution because I'd had such a high-risk pregnancy with Braylin. I guess it was good thing I had already resigned from the bank. Plus, both of our Chryslers had been repossessed and I noticed Hayden was coming home less and less. He still had his Ford Ranger and we went and purchased a white 2003

Ford Explorer with a third row of seating. He said that work was finally picking up and he had several extra loads to take during the week. My husband did have an outstanding work ethic, but I could always tell when he was omitting pertinent information from me. I don't even think he realized he started coming home talking about some new truck driver by the name of Candy. I would just listen and let him ramble on and on about her. She became a regular topic of discussion in our marriage; he had even started grooming and dressing up a little more for work. He also did not realize how often he would say that he could not wait for me to meet her and he had invited her to come visit our church. Honestly, at first I thought nothing of it.

On the morning of May 21, 2007, I woke up feeling strong, frequent contractions and Hayden drove me to the hospital immediately. For some reason, I felt the baby coming out much more than the other three. I could feel such excruciating pain that the nurse gave me some medicine to take the edge off. But the edge still felt pretty sharp to me! It felt like two people had taken each of my legs and ran in opposite directions. It did not help that my doctor and the nurses were busy discussing their plans for the weekend while I was screaming my head off.

I was only in labor for about an hour total! I gave birth to another beautiful baby girl named London Tatum. She was six pounds, seven ounces and she had a head full of curly hair. Hayden left the room immediately after he cut the umbilical cord, saying that he was going to tell our families the baby had been born. He was gone for quite some time, and he finally returned but said he had decided to go home so he could get the children. He had never left me at the hospital overnight by myself before after I gave birth; and from my understanding, the children were going to be staying with Martha so I confronted him about his actions. He insisted that his mom could not keep Miracle, Christian and Braylin and that he needed to go get them.

I went into tubal ligation surgery later that evening and when I finally made it out of recovery and to my hospital room, Daddy and my Momma and a few others had arrived. But I was very lethargic from the anesthesia. Momma asked if I wanted her to stay with me since Hayden was leaving and I declined because he should have been there for me. He obviously had another agenda up his sleeve, knowing I could not come home for the next two days. It was rather eerie staying there alone for two nights, but I slept most of the time.

The next morning, Hayden brought our other three children to the hospital to see London. Braylin, still being a baby herself, was not very receptive of the new infant who was screaming to the top of her lungs. Hayden had put her aside to pick up London so that made matters much worse and she began to cry also. Hayden tried to warm Braylin up to London and put her within her reach to allow her to rub her new baby sister. She scratched London to the white meat so hard that the scar from the scratch still remains on London's nose to this day. London was bleeding and screaming and I asked Hayden to give her back to me. Braylin was notorious for slapping, she had slapped Miracle, Christian and a few unsuspecting adults. She did not like people in her face, but she was still too small for a spanking so it was hilarious. Thankfully Jonathan and Cindy came by to visit while the babies were crying and Cindy helped me calm Braylin down.

On the morning of my discharge, the photographer came in to take London's newborn pictures. Yolita helped me get her dressed for her close up. I was certainly ready to be discharged and in the comfort of my own home. It was hot outside, so I was able to put London in a window in her bassinet to treat her jaundice. But the warmth of the sun would rock her right to sleep. I used those opportunities to get a quick nap in as well. Hayden was helpful getting the children situated before he went back out on the road that evening. London was a good baby, but she demanded to eat every two hours on the dot. I breast fed with both her and Braylin.

Hayden did what he always did when we were blessed with a new child or a happy moment in our life. He would have these epiphanies about our family and how he wanted us to start over in our marriage. Like a fool in love, I would be so excited and praying maybe this time he would really change. Once, we even tried having special date nights and on one of those occasions, we decided to stay in so he went out and bought date night dishes and I set up a candlelight picnic on our living room floor. I was wearing lingerie and he put on Valentine's Day boxers that I had bought for him years before. We would actually take the initiative to enjoy those rare moments of civilization in our marriage. We were once on such a roll, that I managed to convince him to attend the annual Weekend to Remember Marriage Seminar at The Gaylord Texan Resort. We enjoyed ourselves immensely, learned a great deal about how to have a marriage God's way, and completed the assignments in our workbooks. That retreat gave me hope like never before. I was so desperate for change that I had purchased every book, CD and tape on marriage from a variety of ministries on 90.9 KCBI,

Day Star and TBN; but Hayden refused to engage with me.

The "happy phases" in our life together would usually last about two to three weeks or so, and then he'd settle back into the comfort of his preaching and whoremongering of a double lifestyle. He would always revert back to making the same hurtful, rude, idiotic and disrespectful comments to me and often being very unapologetic for his actions. He expressed to me once that he was purposely rebelling against every effort I was making to make our marriage work and that he refused to read any books or listen to a CD on the topic of marriage.

After London had reached about two months old, she was sleeping a little longer and while all of the children were napping one afternoon, Hayden and I sat down to talk. He began his usual run down of the woes of the trucking industry, parts, driver payroll, labor and low-paying loads. From there, the conversation shifted to our monthly bills and cutting costs. Our lights had recently been disconnected because Hayden said he lost the money order to pay the bill. He had been careless with our money before by leaving the money order at the register and of course when he went back the clerk told him he never left it. But this was the first time we'd been without lights. We bathed the kids and ate KFC for dinner by candlelight. We sat down and started mapping out a plan to catch up on our bills, yet again, because everything was always so far behind that Yolita had written Hayden a $10,000 check to bring our mortgage current twice. I was grateful for her help, but tried to talk her out of it simply because I knew if she kept doing that, Hayden would continue to use her as a crutch.

While we were trying to save money, we purchased minutes for our Boost Mobile phones and my minutes were lasting two weeks longer than Hayden's. He had mentioned that his Uncle Dan, one of Pastor Tatum's younger brothers who also happened to be a truck driver, was calling him every day because he had recently been sick. His uncle does like to talk and ramble for a while once he gets going, but I was hoping he was feeling better. About a week later, our phone bill was due and I logged onto the computer to pay and in doing so, I pulled up the statement. I saw a number with the area code 817 showing up on the bill about fourteen times a day. I thought, *man, he does talk to Uncle Dan quite often*. I dialed the number to say hello to Dan and to ask if he was feeling better. But to my surprise, a female voice answered!

"Hi, may I speak to Dan?" I said. The lady replied saying that I had dialed the wrong number. So I asked if she knew Hayden and she said, "Yes" very confidently. Then I asked who she was and she replied, "You need to ask him who I am," and she hung up the phone!

I was seething with rage! I paced the entire first floor of our house while trying to get Hayden on the phone. But he was outside of the calling area so I could not get through. Next, I called Lanitra and began to vent and reiterate the blatant disrespect I had just experienced over the phone with yet another random home-wrecking pigeon. Lanitra was floored and agreed that I should definitely confront Hayden about the mysterious heathen he had been conversing with fourteen times a day.

I remember being so angry that I told her, "He's not even cute enough to keep cheating on me and putting me through hell!"

Of course after this drama presented itself, I was obligated to take a closer look at our phone bills and saw that they had been conversing for several months and always from the time he left for work until right before he was due back home. He had the audacity to call her five minutes after I gave birth to London! *Why did this vulture need a play by play of the intimate details of my labor and delivery?* I also noticed he called her every time he left my hospital room and right before coming to visit me.

Finally, Hayden was calling on my other line and I hung up with Lanitra. I clicked over so fast I don't even think I gave her an opportunity to finish saying goodbye!

"Hey baby, what's up?" he said.

"What's up is you and whoever this woman is that you have been talking to fourteen times a day from an 817 number!"

"Nikki, that's just my friend, Candy."

"Well, I'm your wife and we barely speak during the day. You hardly ever call me and every time I call, you rush me off the phone in less than five minutes. If she's just a friend, what could y'all possibly be talking about so frequently?"

"She's nobody, Nikki; don't trip! I minister to her because she's going through some personal things in her family and she will ask me a question about her big rig sometimes. I've helped her fix a few things on it before. So if it runs funny, she'll call and ask me what she should do. I have to go...my dispatcher is on the other line."

"I'll hold," I said.

But once he was done speaking to the other caller, he disconnected the line. I would not be surprised if it was really Candy calling and he wanted to get the scoop on our brief conversation. I tried calling him back and could not get an answer. When he finally made it home, it was after midnight and I was restless. By that time, I had thought of so many questions and scenarios that just were not adding up. But he refused to talk to me about her.

"She's just a friend and I'm not gone stop talking to her for you!" he said, piercing my heart even more!

I pleaded with Hayden to just answer my questions, but he ignored me, took a shower and went to lie down for a few hours. I sat up crying and feeling very unloved and stupid for getting pregnant three times by the same fool! I had no idea what to do at that point in my marriage. Things were so bad between us that our sex life was almost obsolete. We were no longer heart connected. There was no trust; and honestly, I didn't even desire him anymore. If he fell asleep on the couch, I would sneak past him and go to bed to avoid him touching me. Knowing he was touching someone else when he was away from home made my skin crawl at the thought of him touching me. I would turn the TV off and cover him with a blanket to keep him comfortable down stairs for as long as possible, and if he did come to bed, I would pretend to be asleep.

About two weeks later, Hayden came home really late saying that the big truck broke down and he had been on the side of the road for hours. He seemed to be so tired that he fell right off to sleep after his shower and I grabbed his cell phone to look through it. As soon as I pulled up his text messages, there was a picture of his penis that he had sent to his "friend" Candy. I lost it! I chunked the phone so hard that it accidentally hit him in the chin, but I was not remorseful at all. He woke up dazed and confused, but not baffled enough to be oblivious to what was transpiring in our bedroom. He lied, saying that he took the picture, but decided not to send it and he did the promise song and dance that he always did when he was busted. He went on to say that he would get his number changed again and stop talking to her. He did admit that they talked about me mostly and he said that she was a better listener than I was. She never disagreed with him and that they were engaged in an emotional affair, but they had never had sex. I wanted to choke him!

I replied, "Of course she listens to you and never disagrees, she's never been choked, hit, cheated on, or lied to by you. Not to mention the fact that she's never been kicked out of a house with you, had several cars repossessed with you, raised your children alone, or had to deal with yo negative Momma and the constant interferences of other women and your worldly desires! No one sends a picture of their genitals if there is no sex involved. I would not be surprised if you had her in my house while I was recovering from giving birth to your third child."

"I would never do that to you, Nikki," he shouted, "I love you!"

I went upstairs and cried my eyes out! I just could not believe he really expected to continue to treat me like dirt and get away with it. I had prayed numerous times for God to show him the error of his ways, and for him to reap what he had sown. But I refused to play Russian roulette with my life by having sex with him knowing he had been unfaithful to me. I knew he was not smart enough to protect himself, let alone me.

CHAPTER NINE

Where am I?

After yet another display of infidelity in my marriage, I sank deeper into an already dark and gloomy depression. So dark that I found myself sleeping the days away in hopes that one day I would decide to return to civilization and my life would somehow be much better. I would cry uncontrollably for many hours throughout the day and even though I would bathe the children and make sure they ate, I was not eating at all and rarely bathing. As OCD as I am, I knew something was deeply wrong; but I was at a loss on where to begin repairing me.

I remember climbing on top of a very tall armoire, taking pictures of our room, and then sitting n Braylin and London's room on the floor just staring at the wall for six hours straight one day. I was so overwhelmed that I did not even realize that much time had gone by. I found myself sitting on the floor at the opening of the hallway in our master suite staring at him once while he was asleep and thinking of ways to kill him; then my thoughts shifted to just killing myself.

I was plagued with foreboding thoughts and believed that if I committed suicide, I would finally be with the one and only person who truly loved me and that was Jesus Christ. Satan had waged a furious war on my mind and for a while, he thought he had won! *But God!* The Bible says that faith comes by hearing and though I was quite out of focus, I know God kept me going! I was still attending church three times a week and I would watch Joyce Meyer and T.D. Jakes frequently or listen to their broadcasts on 90.9 KCBI. I also began seeing Christian Counselor, Barbara Jacobs; but this time by myself. I started out pretty consistently, but it was way out of our budget so my twice-a-week appointments changed to once a week, then twice a month.

My sessions first began with me pouring my life story out to Barbara. Therapy was really helping me release a great deal of the pain and secrets of my childhood and marriage that I had held in for so many years. I began to see a pattern forming in my life. I was molested and I held each incident in for many years. Then, I began to rebel as a teenager, and I had been a victim of domestic violence in my marriage. I held that in for many years as well; but to my surprise, the rebellion was also around the corner even at that point in my life.

After several sessions in therapy, I was diagnosed with Post Traumatic Stress Disorder. It was a form of depression related to my husband's physical, emotional and verbal abuse. I was experiencing dissociative episodes that were not conscious; losing track of myself and reality as a coping mechanism. I had become invisible and reduced to a mere speck living in Hayden's shadow; a second-class citizen in my own home and church. He was the important one; the preacher, the face of the family, and the evil one. It appeared to those on the outside looking in that we had the perfect marriage made in heaven, but we were truthfully living in Hell. I would contribute to this false image by covering the bruises Hayden inflicted on my body with makeup, long sleeves and turtlenecks.

I was always reluctant to call the police when Hayden hit me because I was ashamed; and the times I did call were only to scare him and make him stop acting belligerent. But sadly, I still did not have the courage to leave him. Looking back, I don't think it was a lack of courage as much as it was my mental state at the time. It did not help that I felt like there was truly no one I could rely on and people held us to a whole other level of scrutiny because of his status in the church. Our congregation treated us as if we were to be flawless. They held us up on an unattainable pedestal. This created an inability to have the freedom to be transparent with them because they would tear people down instead of lifting them up in love and encouragement.

The sad reality is that people are hurting; and as humans, we are all imperfect and should not appoint ourselves as judges over the sins of others. The church was very unforgiving of any sin or mistakes made by their peers. When your husband is a Minister, whose going to believe that behind closed doors he is a different human being? I walked on eggshells being married to Hayden, not knowing if the day would turn out good or very bad. He has so many similar symptoms to an individual with bipolar disorder. I kept telling myself that if I just did my part to keep the peace between us, I could make him happy. If I just kept crying out to God and praying for him, Hayden would change and love me again. I explained to Barbara that I played the role of having a perfect marriage so well that no one suspected a thing, except the occasional moments of us arguing in public or around other people. But Hayden was not crazy enough to hit me with people watching. We had decided early on in our marriage that divorce was not an option; and somewhere over the many years of this dysfunctional marriage, I had accepted that maybe what we were going through was just what marriage was about. I deluded myself that marriage just equaled enduring pain and Hell together for the sake of the family. *Boy was I wrong!*

Barbara encouraged me to begin pursing modeling and acting. I took some Glamour Shots and she was over the moon about how they turned out. Then I showed her my video reel. I had done some acting with Fred Hammond and Warehouse Worship. Throwing myself back into the entertainment industry gave me an opportunity to model and be on a television show filmed in Addison, Texas with Director Peter Dunn. He seemed like a nice, upstanding preacher and presented himself as someone just helping people in the industry to reach their goals. I had done a photo shoot with his crew and I told him about my book and how God had shown me that through the writing of this book that He was going to allow me to work with Tyler Perry. I was so excited when Peter mentioned that he had grown up in Louisiana and knew Tyler personally since childhood. I thought, *thank You Lord, I'm finally going to meet Tyler Perry as You promised.*

Peter told Hayden that he needed a copy of an excerpt from my book and $1,500 to turn the book into a play first, under Tyler's direction and then a movie. Hayden had always been supportive of my book and my dreams. Peter then told us he was having meetings with Tyler Perry on my behalf in Los Angeles. I was so through the roof with excitement that I got up and announced the news in church and the people rejoiced! I called Peter one afternoon to see what Tyler thought of the excerpt from my book, and he said that they were still in the meeting but everything was looking great. After that conversation, I could not get in touch with him for the next several weeks. I called, and his wife answered saying that the meeting went very well and Peter would be calling me at the end of the week. I never received a call. I called his answering service and they gave him a message to call me. When I finally saw his name on the caller ID almost a month later, I was pretty sure he had been lying to me so I confronted him. He was so upset that I questioned his integrity that he admitted that he did not know Tyler Perry and if he did, Tyler would not care anything about me, my book or my being molested.

I was hurt and I knew that as bad as we were hurting for money, there was no way in the world we would get that $1,500 back. It's scavengers like Peter Dunn that make it hard for writers, actors and models to trust industry opportunities. However, to this day, I am still believing God by faith and knowing that in His timing I will receive a call from Tyler Perry directly, just like He'd shown me in 2006. Anyone that knows me has heard me raving and planting seeds about meeting Tyler someday and working with him.

I had also been in contact via email with a television show producer around that time and she emailed me about a chance to be on *The Morning Show with Mike and Juliet*. I jumped at the opportunity, but Hayden did not want to go to New York. He complained that we could not afford it and he would be missing money by leaving Texas for a few days. I told him the producers of the show wanted to first fly to our home and shoot a story of our life at home with our children and the drastic state of our finances; and then, they would send me and him on an all-expense paid trip to New York City, with an upscale room in Manhattan and a car service to taxi us around during our visit. I pleaded with him to go and told him maybe this would be the trip we needed to get our marriage back on track. I told him had it not been for me over the course of our marriage, we would not have had any fun or memories taking the children to waterparks and theme parks every summer, or having picnics in the park with them feeding the ducks and flying kites. I did all of the planning for their birthday parties because he would never take the initiative. However, he did attend them and barbecued of course or helped decorate. I just wanted him to see that sometime we had to take leaps of faith in order to enjoy life.

Hayden finally agreed to go with me to New York after agreeing that I was right and work would still be there once we returned. We flew there after they shot the footage of the six of us at home. We had a wonderful time sightseeing and being in the studio on a live set. Hayden was so glad that he had decided to go. Although our marriage and finances were still in the same state when we returned from New York, it felt good to just get away for a few days.

Once we returned home, I started working out again and reading my Bible every morning. Hayden was getting jealous and complaining about my workouts and me reading all the time. I think he was just unsatisfied to see me doing anything besides crying over his stupidity and drama. I had finally begun to change my focus and not worry about him or his whereabouts anymore and he did not like that at all.

In an effort to mend fences and the awkward tension between us,

Hayden invited the kids and me to the car wash one Wednesday afternoon to watch while he washed one of the big trucks. When we arrived, he was just starting to pre-rinse the outside of the rig. I hadn't planned to stay long, so after about fifteen minutes of chit chatting, I told him we were going to get home and get dinner and baths done. But he insisted that we stay and asked if I would help him clean the inside. I agreed and climbed up and started organizing and discarding the papers, fast food containers and log sheets he had scattered about in the front part of the cab. Then, as I was making up the bed, I noticed some underwear and some other items of clothing that obviously belonged to him, but things I had never seen. This made me very uncomfortable and I began to think of all his lies and late arrivals and decided to just go ahead and go home to prevent an argument.

When I climbed down out of the truck he said, "Dang, that was fast!"

I told him what I had done with his papers I had straightened up, and that on second thought, the kids and I should just go ahead and get home so that we can get to Bible Study on time and we would see him later. He said ok and asked why I looked so sad. A million thoughts ran through my mind about his mysterious underwear in answer to that question, but instead I just told him that I was cool and hugged him goodbye.

He reached out for me and said his infamous quote, "Gimme some of dat sugar." I kissed him.

I put the kids into their car seats and seat belts and we drove away. About five minutes down the road, my cell rang and it was Hayden calling us. I thought maybe he was calling to say what he wanted for dinner or how long he'd be before coming home.

"Hello!" I answered.

"Nikki, I ain't no fool. I know why you're upset."

"I'm not upset. I told you I was cool. Why are you trying to start an argument? What's your problem?"

"You didn't leave because you were ready to get the kids home, Nikki! You left because you were being nosey and found my new cell phone!"

I was very perplexed, but I allowed him to continue out of curiosity. He went on to say that he bought a second cell phone and did not tell me about it because he only talks to Candy on it.

"She's a really good friend to me and I refuse to stop talking to her just because you're jealous and insecure!"

I had never been so speechless in my entire life. I screamed, "You idiot! I didn't even see a phone. I saw your new underwear tucked down on the side of the mattress; but thank you for tattling on yourself though!"

He kept going on about how he didn't believe me and defending his relationship with her until the moment I hung up the phone. About ten minutes later, he came home and that argument escalated terribly. It was so bad that I was still crying and upset when we arrived at Bible Study, which at the time was being held at his parent's home. Our old church had been sold and the new church was being built, but we had Sunday school and Morning Worship at a Recreational facility.

Sister Fuller, one of the elderly ladies that I was very close to, saw me upset and came over to console me. That made Martha angry because she had always been jealous of our friendship. So after Bible Study, she told Pastor Tatum he needed to make me and Hayden stay behind for a meeting with the two of them. This so-called "meeting of sincere concern" at first turned into yet another bashing session of three against one. *Guess who the odd man out was? Me!*

Hayden sat quietly with his head down as he had done countless times before, while his parents accused me of being selfish, insecure, jealous and a down-right horrible wife from their one-sided perspectives. Being scolded at almost thirty years of age was starting to get very old for me; so I spoke up for myself and I told them about his strip club obsession, the extra phone, his experimenting with smoking blacks, hidden bank accounts and the hot pink condom. I even explained how I was considerate enough, as a wife, to keep the children quiet while he studied for his sermons in spite of his constant threats to kill me when he was angry.

They were both looking dumbfounded as if their son was incapable of sinning. Pastor Tatum's entire demeanor changed and he let Martha take over the meeting while Hayden reluctantly explained and made excuses for his conduct. I could tell Hayden was completely humiliated and shocked that I had finally told someone something about the real him; and out of all the people in the world, I was telling it to his beloved parents.

Martha still did not believe me; but Pastor Tatum tried to make light of the situation and said to Hayden, "You have a good looking wife and you are not all that in the looks department. It's cheaper to keep her. If I were you, I would straighten up and fly right!"

When Pastor Tatum said that, he and I chuckled so hard, but Martha's mouth fell open and she gave him a look that could kill.

The following Sunday morning, I woke up frightened by a very vivid dream. I scared Hayden when I jumped up. He asked what was wrong and I began to describe my dream to him. I explained that I saw some sort of chaos because people were running all over the place. Then two strong men came and grabbed him by his arms and locked him away in a cage. I had been knocked down on the ground and was struggling to pull myself up from the dirt. Hayden blew me off and said, "It was just a dream, let's get up and get the kids ready so we won't be late for Sunday school."

I got out of bed, made everyone breakfast, and then dressed the kids and myself for church. The six of us rushed out of the door every Sunday morning, running late. We had an awesome service and sang our hearts out in morning worship. I was looking forward to our weekly Sunday dinner and nap routine when Yolita walked over to remind me that she was going to the store to buy Christian and Miracle's school uniforms and supplies. They were entering kindergarten and second grade; their summer was ending that Sunday, and they were excited about the first day of school and going to a new grade.

We piled in the car and followed Yolita and Percy to the Walmart in Cedar Hill. When we arrived, I initially took Braylin and London in a basket to the opposite side of the store because I wanted to kill two birds with one stone and get everything we needed during one trip. As I was browsing, I could hear Hayden yelling at the top of his lungs.

I pushed the kids in the cart down to the other end of the store to see what all of the commotion was about. Hayden was on ten; saying that Miracle was playing in the store and he had to tell her twice to stop running underneath the clothes racks.

"Dang, I really thought something was wrong because we could hear you yelling from the other end of the store!" I said.

He started yelling at me in front of Yolita, Percy and the many other patrons of Walmart on that crowded Sunday afternoon. I told him to stop trying to show out in front of his sister. What Miracle had done could not have been serious enough for him to be yelling across the store!

Yolita and Percy were done getting the children's things and went to check out, but I was still shopping; so after hugging them goodbye and thanking them, I walked away and left Hayden up front to take the children's things to our car. As soon as they left, Hayden came back inside the store looking for us and trying to rehash the entire stupid display of public humiliation. I just kept browsing and walking away from him; refusing to embarrass myself with him.

My actions were making him more and more angry. He got louder and louder. He began tearing through the store like *The Incredible Hulk* going on and on. That day, I had the peace of God and was not in the mood to retaliate and argue with him, so I stayed quiet the entire time. I kept up my silence even as he was still yelling when we reached the checkout, and then all the way home. I still would not say a word. The children and I were just watching him make a fool of himself.

As soon as we walked in the door, I put my purse on the desk in my home office and turned on the computer. Hayden continued ranting and raving and being mean to Miracle and barked at her to go upstairs. Finally, I'd had enough. I told her to come into the office with me and her siblings instead. He got so furious that he walked over to the desk yelling and cursing. He picked up my purse and hit me so hard in my eye with it that it immediately swelled shut. Then he went outside with the garage door still up yelling, cursing and punching the walls. I could feel that something was really wrong with my eye, but I panicked when I rubbed it and had blood on my hands. I went out to the garage to show him what he had done and asked him if he felt better. I asked him if his actions made him feel like a man.

I went back inside to the guest bathroom mirror. The children were screaming and following me, so I took them back into the office and picked up the phone to call the police, but I only had time to dial 91. As soon as I sat down in the chair and picked up the receiver, Hayden came in and flipped me out of the chair. He picked me up and drug me to the chaise by my neck and body slammed me on top of it. I was trying to kick and fight him back, and my babies were begging him to stop hitting me; but he sat on my abdomen and would not get off of me. Christian and Miracle were tugging at his pant leg crying and Braylin and London were screaming.

Suddenly there was a very loud knock at the door. Thank the Lord someone had heard all of the commotion and called the Cedar Hill Police. They immediately made the children go upstairs and Pastor Tatum showed up shortly after Hayden was escorted outside. The children saw Hayden being handcuffed and put into the squad car from the game room window on our second floor, but they did not mention

9

it until later that night.

The other officer took pictures of my eye, torn clothing, and the abrasions on my body while asking me what happened. As I began to explain to him the whole Walmart scenario, Pastor Tatum interrupted to say, "Yeah, but what did you do to make him hit you?"

The officer and I both just stood there in amazement.

"I did not do anything," I tried to explain. "As a matter of fact, I kept walking away from him."

"Well, that's not what Yolita and Percy told me," he said!

I couldn't help but think, *why would you rush over here uninvited if they had not alarmed you in some way.*

The officer then asked Pastor Tatum to step aside and he walked away; but when he returned, I told him that Yolita and Percy were gone before Hayden went completely ape nuts in Walmart.

Pastor Tatum responded, "You never put these people in your business." I tried to explain to him just how sad I was and that I really needed help. "If you're battling with depression and thoughts of suicide, you must not be saved," he said.

At that very moment I felt something in the core of my spirit snap completely in half. I could not believe that my Pastor of the last seven years was actually questioning my belief in Jesus Christ as my Savior, because I was depressed. More importantly, why was he not trying to pray for me or help me heal? Why was he not considering that Hayden needed healing as well and deliverance? I just wanted him to forget for one second that Hayden was his son and for him to see me as a hurting individual; a member of his congregation, a human being, and the mother of his grandchildren who had just witnessed the entire act of violence committed on me by their father , by the way!

My body was so weak as I stood there struggling to see with one eye and waiting for my "Pastor" to take his daddy hat off and show me just one ounce of compassion or love. My Pastor had failed me; but more importantly, he had failed as my friend and the one person I looked up to the most. The emptiness I felt was indescribable! I could have exploded and shattered into a million tiny pieces.

The rest of that night was sad and eerie; it was so surreal for me. After the police took Hayden off to jail and Pastor Tatum left, I collapsed to the floor weeping in deep sorrow. I was very confused at how we could go from a wonderful church service to a horrific extreme. Then as I sat on the floor God allowed me to remember the dream I had earlier that morning before we left for church. I believe it was His way of warning me, prophetically, about the events that were to take place that day.

I called Carl to tell him that his best friend had been hauled off to jail. He and his girlfriend, Isis, rushed right over and stayed up talking with me downstairs in the den until about 2:00 a.m. They slept over downstairs. I went up to bed until time for the children to get up, but I could not fall off to sleep. Hayden called earlier that night from jail cursing and blaming me for his being locked up. He screamed and talked about how much he hated me for causing him to go to jail. I tried to tell him that I never dialed 911 and that the neighbors must have heard him shouting and slamming doors and called the police. I was so hurt that he actually blamed me for his stupidity and senseless actions that I just hung up the phone. The next morning, Carl and Isis helped me get my babies up and off for their first day of school.

After I returned, Hayden called; but this time, he was singing a different tune. Homeboy was crying and apologizing left and right! He said he was mad when he called the night before because he had never been to jail before and he was scared. I guess sitting in jail can change a person's perspective. He stayed in jail for one night because Yolita was not going to allow him to stay much longer than that. Their entire family always looked to her for financial support, so it did not surprise me one bit. Unfortunately, that was part of Hayden's problem; he'd been spoiled and enabled for his entire life and he could not stand on his own two feet as an adult.

A few days later, Yolita and Pastor Tatum came over to check on me and the children. My eye was still patched up, but that conversation was totally avoided; however, I did appreciate the fact that they thought enough of us to come by. I did not get a phone call or visit from Martha, my "first lady"! After they left, I called my good friend, Monica Dailey, and she rushed right over when she heard the pain in my voice as I was trying to explain the recent events. She and I had been friends since late 2003 when we worked at Aetna together. Over the years, Monica had provided me with a great deal of pointers on cooking and being a good mother and a wife. I was thankful for her resourcefulness, concern, and tenacity to always have my back as a big sister when push came to shove.

She assured me that Hayden got what he deserved for flying into a rage and that my children and I were going to be okay regardless of the outcome. It was a message of empowerment and I held on to her words. I can remember rejoicing in the moment and the very things she had spoken over me and my children began to come true.

Once Hayden was released, the judge ordered him not to return home. Of course, he was going to stay with his Momma until the court order expired. The children and I had so much peace while he was away for those weeks. However, it was very awkward seeing him and his family at church. He would not talk to me; only the babies; and quite honestly, I was fine with that because it may have just escalated into another grand argument if he did. I guess he was recanting the apology from jail. The explosive display of our marriage was the beginning of its complete end, but Hayden's attitude finally changed when he was tired of being away from home.

He was calling me constantly; apologizing and spouting out the usual promises to change his terrible attitude and behavior. He was suddenly ready to work diligently on saving our marriage. I was either too nice and forgiving, or stupid enough to believe him. I went to the police station to sign an affidavit allowing the judge to drop the charges and order him to six months of mandatory anger management instead and he was then allowed to come back home. We started out as usual when we were trying to patch things up between us and move forward. We sat and talked and listened to one another's concerns. He changed his phone number for the thousandth time to work on rebuilding trust. We read the Bible and marriage books together for all of about three to six weeks before familiarity reared its ugly head again. But unbeknownst to either of us, this time things would turn out extremely different.

CHAPTER TEN

Through the Fire, I walked

All of the stress I was going through was certainly a major setback for me mentally. I was not completely out from underneath the dark cloud over my life; not even close. I just wished I could have afforded to continue to go to therapy frequently, because I still found myself struggling at home. In 2008, Pastor Tatum told me one Sunday as we were leaving Cheddars in Grand Prairie, that God told him that I was speaking, but no one was listening. I believe God was trying to reveal to him then, that I had been crying out for years and that my husband and I were in drastic need of spiritual help and prayers. But he was also letting it be known that I had been constantly disregarded.

I started working at Quest Diagnostics in the same office with Martha. It was an awesome job because I was allowed to work the hours of my choice as long as I completed forty hours a week. Being a mom, this was a win-win situation for me to have the ability to come to work as early as 3:00 a.m. and get off at 1:00 p.m. I could only work that early when Hayden took a load late enough to drop the kids off at school and daycare; but I enjoyed each opportunity I got. The office was so casual and laid-back that I would listen to my radio or a DVD movie while working, so the time went by rather quickly every day. Some good things really are too good to be true. The pitfall of that experience was that I felt like Martha and I were still living under the same roof because I saw her so much.

After a while of being around her Monday through Friday, working ten-hour days and at church with her three times a week, it was becoming a bit overwhelming for me in conjunction with the drama I was dealing with concerning her son. I had become very withdrawn and started slowly giving myself the space I needed. I began visiting *The Potter's House* on Wednesdays with my dearly departed friend, Patrice Williams. I even cut back on a few of Hayden's family gatherings and began to stay home more, and for the first time in a long time, I felt like this was ok. Hayden and I were usually tied to each other's hips at all times, so I welcomed the breathing room that I was experiencing.

Martha and Pastor Tatum were not pleased with me missing church; but at least I was still in The Lord's house to sing in the choir on Sunday mornings. Not only was Martha the biggest gossip in the church, she would also tell all of the church and her husband's business while she was at work. I realized quickly just how much my coworkers had heard about my marriage along with several other inappropriate topics of discussion Martha had been engaging in. The knowledge of how lose her lips were made me feel very guarded and uncomfortable with the morale at the work place.

I had recently been complaining to my closest friends – Lanitra and Hayden's cousin, Kinea Smith – that I felt trapped; stuck in an unfulfilling life and claustrophobic. So, what transpired next should have been no surprise to either one of them. But no one knew I had been seeking professional counseling for all of the stress from my husband and his family. I was not out of the woods in my recovery process of being mentally and spiritually healthy when I discovered that Barbara's office had suddenly closed. I'm not sure why, but when I drove by one day headed to the store, I noticed a leasing sign in the window and the curtains were gone. The building was completely empty. I felt like a rug had been ripped from underneath my feet! It was very discouraging because I believed she was helping me so much that I was almost at the cusp of just a little more understanding of my life and how to navigate from where I was to where I needed to be in order to maintain my sanity. I am not crazy; I am pragmatic! But Hayden was determined to make all of the people he could convince to believe otherwise. I was certainly going to miss my sessions with Barbara and tried to hold on to all of the tools and advice she had provided.

I remembered that Barbara had also challenged me to confront all of my demons and one of them was Rodney Hall, Miracle's father. I never spoke of him and certainly never thought of him. I cringed at the thought of him being a regular part of Miracle's life as soon as Barbara suggested it. He was so selfish and irresponsible; plus, he had signed his parental rights of her over to Hayden when she was four. But Barbara thought it would be a good idea for Miracle to still have an opportunity to meet him at some point; especially since she had gotten a little older and could possibly understand the situation a little bit better. I was so reluctant to comply with Barbara's request that I did not even entertain the thought until two years later in early 2009 because I detested Rodney and what he done to Miracle and me in 1999. Ten years had not lessened the pain. The only reason I remembered Barbara's advice was because I noticed Hayden was becoming increasingly hard on Miracle; just down right mean and rude to her. She was only nine years old and he was acting as if he and Miracle were the same age, but he never reprimanded our other three children. The funny thing is she's so sweet she would just continue loving on him no matter how bad he treated her compared to the others.

I had the notion that maybe Barbara was right, and maybe Miracle did have the right to finally know the truth about her biological father. Hayden knew I was considering the thought of allowing some sort of relationship between Rodney and Miracle, and he did not have a problem with it. But when I mentioned the idea to Martha one day at work, she disagreed completely. I even tried to explain to her how Hayden was treating Miracle and being mean toward her, but she wouldn't hear it. She handled it as she had done every other serious conversation I tried over the years to have with her, by blowing me off and jokingly saying she would kick Hayden's butt if he ever mistreated Miracle. I was looking for some adult advice from someone who had refused for so many years to give me any guidance. I regret ever asking her anything and wasting my time! But it was my own fault because I kept trying to give her the benefit of the doubt, hoping someday she would go back to being the cool lady I became friends with in 2000 when we first met. *Silly me!* It was just another failed attempt at getting her to see how she could have been a role model and positive influence in my life instead of an additional thorn in my side. Even Pastor Tatum called me into his study one Sunday morning to apologize to me for his wife not being the example to me that she should be. I really appreciate that he not only noticed, but was humble enough to say something.

I needed a second opinion from someone who knew firsthand what I had experienced when Rodney abandoned me and my child all those years ago. I called Monique and I love talking to her because she always gives her honest opinion. By that time, Monique was a police officer. She was very upset to hear how Hayden had been mistreating Miracle and although she could not stand him, she volunteered to find Rodney for me. I was shocked when she called back the next day with his cell number, but I was still afraid to dial it. My fear of the unknown concerning Rodney was magnified when Monique added the tidbit of information that he had been a witness to a recent altercation and his number was taken down by one of the officers who responded to the call.

I took it all in; not knowing what to think. I didn't know how Miracle would process the news about her father or how any of it would make her feel. I thought long and hard about opening a door when I really did not know what was on the other side of it. So, instead of calling Rodney, first I pulled out his old folder containing our court order for visitation and his child support responsibilities which was over $40,000 in arrears. The folder had an old photo of him that I had kept for her over the years, knowing that sooner or later the day would come when I might need it, but never really knowing when that day would come.

All of the children were upstairs playing and I called Miracle into my closet. I asked her to sit down on the closet floor with me so we could talk. This is where I spend most of my time praying and reading my Bible, so I asked her to come in there just in case she wanted to cry, pray or anything else. I really could not prepare myself for what her response would be. I began by telling her the story about Jesus and Joseph and how Joseph was responsible for being Jesus' earthly father, but that God was His father. I used this as a way to give her a foundation for her to understand where I was coming from. Then I told her that Hayden was kind of like Joseph to her and that he was not her biological father. The look on her face in that moment was one I have ever regretted seeing on the face of any of my children. I could tell that a huge wave of emotion came upon her. I sat quietly watching her little mind process what I was trying to convey. She was hurt and confused, yet extremely curious.

She asked, "Well, If Daddy is not my real Daddy, then who is?" I pulled Rodney's picture from the folder and showed it to her and she began to cry. Her next questions were, "Where is he and why hasn't he been here?"

I hugged her and told her that I didn't know where he was and asked if she wanted to meet him and ask him those questions for herself. I reminded her that I had always been there for her in the past and that I would always be there for her in the future. I added that she was blessed to have Hayden in her life also. At first she was obviously angry and she sat with her back against the wall engulfed in her own little world of thought.

After a few moments of silence, she responded, "Yes, Mommy, I want to meet Rodney. I have so many questions for him."

"I understand, baby and hopefully you will get to ask him anything you want to; but don't get your hopes up yet, let me see if I can get in contact with him first."

She went back to playing with the other children in the game room and I went downstairs to dial Rodney's number. I exhaled deeply as I dialed the number and the phone rang twice. A woman answered and I asked to speak to Rodney.

"He's not here," she said in a very friendly voice. I was surprised that not once did she inquire about who I was, given the fact that I was another female calling her home. I thanked her and we hung up. I waited until the next morning before calling back and the same woman answered; but this time, she said, "Hold on."

I could hear her telling Rodney to get the phone. My heart sank. I was actually going to get to talk to him after all those years. I could not believe Monique had found him so easily.

He finally came to the phone and said, "Hello, who is this?"

"Hi, Rodney Hall, it's me Nikki!"

"Nikki? Quee!"

"Yes, It's me, how are you?"

"I'm good, but I work nights, so let me call you back in a few hours when I get up."

"Cool," I said and I hung up!

You would think when you have a child with someone and you have not heard from or seen them in years, your first response would be what's up or where's my baby...etcetera. *But no!* Not Rodney, he was talking to me like he hadn't missed a beat in Miracle's life. He hadn't changed a bit.

I didn't want to mention to Miracle that I talked to him yet. However, she had gone into the game room and told Christian, Braylin and London all about Rodney. I walked into a room full of faces filled with curiosity. Because of that, I had to explain to them what Miracle was talking about. Christian was eight, so he could sort of grasp the whole story, but Braylin and London were only three and two at the time, so they didn't really get it.

Later that afternoon, Rodney called back and when he asked for Quee, I knew it was him.

"Long time, no see or hear from you," I said sarcastically.

He replied, "Yeah, I know. I've been busy, but what's up?"

"I want Miracle to meet you!" I said with absolutely no expectation because I knew how selfish Rodney was as a person.

"Why, Quee? The last time I saw you, you were bragging about how your husband was taking care of her and how you didn't need me."

"Don't act like I was keeping Miracle from you because of Hayden. Rodney, she's not wanting for anything; trust me on that! I just want her to meet you now that she's old enough to have a better understanding of where she came from. I told her about you for the first time yesterday because, of course, she didn't know who you were at the park five years ago."

He changed his tone and then became his usual comical self. He started asking me what I had been up to and, of course, I lied and painted a happily married picture because it would have been inappropriate for me to disclose the truth. We talked on the phone and reminisced about people we'd known mutually and how our old boss, Steve, had passed away. We continued on for a while just chatting like old friends.

When Miracle came downstairs, I asked him if he wanted to talk to her and he said he was nervous and that he didn't know what to say. But I told her it was Rodney on the phone and gave her the phone anyway before he could weasel out of talking to her.

She said hello and I could hear him asking her how she was, about school and her plans for the summer. She talked to him as if they had already established a rapport. He asked her if she could sing and told her that her other sisters could sing well. She said yes and began to sing Celine Dion's song, "Because You Loved Me." Then she became quiet and shy and handed me the phone.

He said, "Quee, she has a beautiful voice but did she say I'm everything I am because you left me?"

I laughed so hard and replied, "You are so dumb, she said because you 'loved' me silly. Have you ever heard the song?" I was too tickled!

I asked him when Miracle was going to get to get a chance to see him because now that they had talked, I knew that she was going to keep asking me about seeing him. I think he was more afraid of seeing her face to face than he had been when I put her on the phone. At first he started making excuses. I told him how I didn't have time for the runaround. I did not want to get her hopes up if he was not really going to show up. He said he didn't know when, but to let him think about a good time and he would call me the next day to talk about it more. After that, we hung up.

When Hayden came in that evening, he said he and Christian were going fishing in the morning. I knew Christian would enjoy that and the girls and I could hang out together while the two of them were gone. I told Hayden about Rodney's call and that he said he would call back to set up a time and place to meet Miracle. I also let Hayden know that I did not want Rodney coming to our home, so I thought maybe a meeting in the park again would be the way to go about it. Hayden said that he thought it was good that Miracle had gotten a chance to talk to Rodney, but he wanted to talk to Rodney himself just to make sure that he understood that we were not asking Rodney for anything for Miracle except for his time. I agreed with him. I just did not want my daughter to get hurt in any way.

That Saturday morning, on June 6, 2009, Rodney called saying he had a detailing business on the side and he was going to be close to Cedar Hill at a car wash in Duncanville on Wheatland Road He asked if Miracle and I could meet him there. I told him to let me see and I would call him back in a few minutes. I called Hayden because he and Christian had left before daybreak to go fishing. I wanted to make sure he did not have any problems with me taking Miracle to the car wash. When I told him about Rodney's call, he said it was cool for the girls and me to take Miracle to meet Rodney at the car wash.

He jokingly said, "You should make him detail your truck for free while he's at it, that's the least he can do."

We both laughed and I hung up to call Rodney back to confirm the time. The girls and I arrived at the car wash on time; however, Rodney was over thirty minutes late. I was furious and thinking he was not going to show because at first he would not answer his phone, and then when he did answer, he kept saying he was almost there. Miracle was so excited but yet very nervous to meet him because she's so shy and I did not want him to let her down.

We'd been sitting in the truck parked in the shade while we waited for him, so I let the girls out of their car seats. Miracle became sad while we waited when I told her maybe we should leave and try again another day. Just as I was about to get out and buckle them back up, Rodney pulled up to the car vacuums in front of us.

I turned to Miracle and said, "There he is."

She was acting as if she was about to meet her favorite boy band; she was elated! When he got out of his car and started walking toward my truck Miracle said, "He looks just like me!"

I laughed. The four of us got out of the truck and headed toward Rodney. He picked Miracle up and gave her a big hug. *She was over the moon!* I introduced him to Braylin and London and he said how cute they were and that I looked good too.

"You still look the same," I said to him as I took him in visually from head to toe.

"Dang!" he said jokingly as we both laughed "Can I detail your car for you?"

"Yeah, but I'm not paying for it," I responded with my eye brows raised.

Rodney smiled and started washing my truck. There was a lot of Saturday morning traffic at the car wash, so the girls and I just hung out until he was done vacuuming the inside. I told him I wanted us to go somewhere so he could talk to Miracle in a little more private setting. I let him know that she had quite a few unanswered questions for him, and with the loud music, the wind, and the crowd, the car wash just did not seem like the best place for her to get answers.

He agreed and followed us to a park in Cedar Hill. While we were driving to the park, Hayden called and said he and Christian were on their way back from fishing and I told him which park we were headed to.

When we arrived at the park, Rodney pulled some brushes from his trunk and continued detailing the inside of my Explorer and the girls ran to play on the swings. We were there for maybe twenty minutes before Rodney was pushing Miracle on the swings and talking to her alone. Braylin, London and I were sitting in the shade playing. Then Rodney came back to my truck to finish working on it, when Hayden pulled up next to the truck. Hayden got out of his truck and introduced himself to Rodney. This is the very first time the two men had ever laid eyes on each other and they were both very guarded. I could tell Hayden was peacocking for Rodney; he had his chest stuck out as he reiterated that we were not looking for any financial support from him, but that it would be nice for Miracle to spend some time with him and to get to know her many other siblings and family members.

Hayden's tone came off as if he was scolding him, so Rodney, being an alpha male, was still very skeptical of Hayden's actions so he did not say very much during their conversation.

Rodney ended up doing such a wonderful job detailing my car, that Hayden asked him to detail the Ram as well. Rodney responded by saying that he would do it, but that he needed access to soap and water in order to do it right. Hayden was still trying to show off, so he got the not so bright idea to invite Rodney over to our home to do the detailing. I thought this was strange so after Rodney and the children were all inside the car, I asked Hayden why he would invite Rodney into our home.

"Don't worry about it, I got this!" he said as he closed the door behind me.

I think he just wanted to show off our house that we were so far behind on in payments...yet again. Just like I knew that he just had to come to the park to floss for Rodney in his new Dodge Ram truck. Everything in me knew that the trip to our house was not a good idea.

After arriving home from the park, the three of us parked in the back and the children ran into the backyard to play. Rodney left the music on playing John P. Kee, as he prepared soap and water to use to wash Hayden's truck. Hayden asked Rodney about the CD and began making small talk about the choir he used to sing with at Kimball High School. He heard Rodney singing and started acted as if he was a fan. I'd never seen a man fall all over another man like that before; not a heterosexual man anyway.

After the obvious tension and anxiety subsided between the two of them, Hayden and Rodney began talking as if they were old college roommates. Rodney finally began to open up to Hayden because Hayden had been boosting his ego. The three of us were in the driveway laughing and talking, but once Rodney started to reminisce about how he and I were musically inclined and mentioning the music we listened to back in the day, Hayden became very uncomfortable. It was obvious that he felt out of place watching us laugh, especially in areas where he was being left out of the conversation. *An unintentional third wheel of sorts!*

Hayden began making weird facial expressions and he finally called me over to him while Rodney was retrieving something from his trunk.

"Nikki, why are you out here?" he asked.

"What do you mean? He's Miracle's dad and he doesn't know you from a can of paint; so why wouldn't I be out here?"

"Well, I don't feel comfortable with you being out here; I can talk to him by myself."

"Cool, I don't have a problem with that, but if you were going to be uncomfortable about it, you should have never invited him over here in the first place. That's exactly what I was saying to you as you were trying to showcase to him about all that you've been doing for Miracle over the years."

"I'm not showcasing! I'm just sizing the man up."

"Whatever," I said as I walked into the house.

I was curious to see what Hayden was up to and why he was acting so suspicious and eager to get Rodney alone to himself. I went inside and fed the children some lunch and once that was out of the way, I went upstairs to Miracle's room over the garage and let up her window. I could hear the two of them talking, but once again, when Rodney addressed me through the window, Hayden got upset again, so I let the window down and went to watch television.

Martha came by to drop off Jada, Hayden's niece. Rodney was at our house at least five hours that day as he and Hayden were outside talking and listening to CDs. When he was done detailing Hayden's filthy truck, Rodney came inside to wash his brushes. Hayden paid Rodney for the work he had done on both trucks and Rodney told Miracle bye and gave her a big hug.

"Bye, Rodney," Miracle said with a wave.

Hayden got upset and tried to correct the way she had addressed him, but Rodney told him it was ok, he understood. He then turned to me and said he would start coming to get her to spend time with her and he got in his car and drove away.

As soon as Rodney drove off, Hayden started saying how cool Rodney was and that he was entirely different from what he had imagined him to be over the years. I think Hayden was more star struck than Miracle over meeting Rodney.

"Hayden, how did you go from not ever wanting to meet him to this?"

"I'm a pretty good judge of character and I know a good dude when I see one. We talked mostly about the Bible and all of the Gospel artists."

I reminded him that Rodney was well versed in the Bible, but he was also the biggest con artist in Texas and he could swoon anyone with his lingo and swagger.

"Don't trust him as far as you can throw him," I warned. "He's very crafty and charismatic."

Hayden got defensive and said, "Me and Rodney are cool and you need to give me his number because he left his plastic water bottle that he used for detailing in the kitchen."

I went upstairs and began giving the children their baths and getting our Sunday clothes out for church. I rolled my eyes thinking, *why does Hayden have such a man crush on Rodney?* While I was getting the children ready for bed, Miracle told me that Rodney explained to her that he had been absent in her life because he was overseas playing basketball and singing on tour. It took everything in me not to burst out in laughter! I could not believe that was the explanation he came up with after all these years to give to his daughter about why he had been absent from her life. He had always been such an elaborate liar, but this was team too much!

Hayden went through my phone and got Rodney's number while we were upstairs and as I was getting ready for bed, he mentioned that he was going to call Rodney the next day. I never said a word. I turned off the light, crawled into bed, and went to sleep.

A few weeks had past and Miracle had not heard from Rodney yet. Hayden and I had gotten into an argument one Friday morning over his normal foolishness and disrespectful verbal abuse and belittling. I left the house to prevent things from escalating and went to the Whataburger on Camp Wisdom where one of my little brothers was working at the time. I talked to him for a short while and my cell phone rang as I was leaving the parking lot. It was Rodney asking where I was.

"Why?" I asked.

"I just got off the phone with Hayden. He called me to talk about the argument the two of you had."

I was shocked and completely embarrassed that Hayden had called Rodney to talk about our marriage. Prior to that, I had been building Hayden up to Rodney for all these years, and now Hayden was revealing to Rodney how much of a shell of a man that he really was.

What *grown man calls his wife's ex to discuss his marriage?* I couldn't help thinking that as Rodney continued to talk.

"Quee, can I come meet you?" he said.

"Yeah, I'm in Duncanville off of Camp Wisdom and Hillside."

"Okay, cool. I'm in the area; meet me at Lakeside Park around the corner from where you are in fifteen minutes and we can talk."

I was reluctant to meet with him, but very curious to know why Hayden would call him to air our dirty laundry and to see what was really going on. Rodney and I pulled into the park and he got out of his car and got into my truck all chipper.

"What's up, Queebie?"

"You tell me," I said.

He asked me why Hayden kept calling him and I said, "What do you mean?"

He says, Quee, he has called me several times this week and today when he called, he was talking about you and saying how his momma don't like you and you don't trust him and that you're evil and very jealous."

I sat there thinking to myself, *first of all, why would my supposed husband be telling my ex all of these lies about me and secondly, this man cannot be lying on Hayden because he knows too much about my marriage.* I told Rodney that Hayden had taken his number from my phone and was supposed to be calling him about his water bottle that he had left behind a few weeks ago.

"Nawh, Quee...his niece was outside at y'all's house when he was talking bad about you the first day I met him, you can ask her."

"No wonder he was so anxious for me to go inside," I said. "Jada is a child and I just cannot believe that he could do me like that in front of her. Why would he be discussing our marriage with you?"

"I know, Queebie...man, and this dude is different! I don't want to call him gay, but he's not like any of the cats I hang with, he's just different, Quee!" Rodney went on to say that he counsels women in broken marriages on the side.

"How are you a bouncer at night and a counselor 'slash' car detail person by day?" I said. We both laughed and started talking and catching up. I was left with no choice but to fill him in on my marriage because my husband had already opened that door by lying and telling everything in a one-sided way.

Rodney and I sat at the park talking for at least two hours. From that day forward, we began to talk on a regular basis and my marriage troubles and Miracle became the topic of discussion every time we spoke. He would also give me regular updates about his conversations with Hayden which were becoming more frequent.

One Sunday evening after church, Hayden left for work to drop off a load. I thought to myself that he must have been going pretty far for him to have left so early. At about 8:00 p.m., my phone rang and it was Rodney. He said he was just checking on me and wanted to see if I was okay and that he was concerned about things between Hayden and me. I told him I was good, and that Hayden was at work and I was chillin downstairs watching a movie. He said Hayden was still blowing his phone up talking bad about me and he was asking me what I was going to do.

"What do you mean? I don't know what to do at this point; my marriage was terrible long before now."

Someone was calling his name in the background so he had to get off of the phone. "Quee, I'm working at the club tonight so I'll call you later."

I said, "Ok," and we hung up.

When I hung up the phone all I could think is, *Wow! How can Hayden be so conniving and not only lie, but tell only one side of the story? More importantly, why is he so driven to make everyone believe that I am such a vicious woman?*

I didn't even bother calling Hayden to confront him at that moment. We had already been arguing about him calling Rodney and putting him in our business, so I just didn't feel like adding more to it at that time. I put the kids to bed and fell asleep watching TV downstairs. The phone rang and woke me up at about midnight.

"Hello!" I said.

"Quee, can I come by?"

"Come by? Do you know what time it is and for what?"

"So we can talk. I didn't really get a chance to talk to you earlier!"

"I don't think that's a good idea, Rodney. My husband is at work and my children are asleep."

"I won't stay long, Quee. Just let me come by and chill with my homie for a lil bit, please."

Reluctantly, I finally said ok and I knew it was wrong to let him come by so late, but I was curious to hear more about what else Hayden could still possibly be telling him. I told him to barely knock on the door when he came so that the children would not wake up. He parked a few streets over and walked to our house. I let him in through the garage and all I could hear were his dress shoes tapping down the hardwood of my hallway floor. He was dressed to the nine and smelling so wonderful! He came through the door with a drink in his hand, sat it down, and gave me a big hug.

"Dang, Quee…man, why didn't you tell me you had it rough in your marriage?"

"Because that's not something you and I, nor you and Hayden, should be discussing, let's go sit down in the den."

He sat on the chaise and I sat on the couch over by the back door. "Quee, Hayden was throwing you under the bus! What happened? How did y'all get there because when I saw you at the park years back, you had nothing but good things to say about this dude? You were bragging about how good of a husband and daddy he was, so what went wrong, Queebie?"

Hayden had opened up a door that he would never be able to close again. I was furious, but yet still calm. I went ham as Rodney sat there listening attentively. I divulged every gory detail of my eight years of being married to the biggest idiot on the planet earth. We talked for hours again about Martha, Hayden's violent behavior, his infidelity, and the whole nine yards. Rodney was seemingly shocked and puzzled at why I had stayed so long, especially after being driven to the point of suicidal thoughts and depression.

As we sat there talking, all of the memories of our relationship started flooding back and we realized that after breaking up ten years ago, we had never gotten closure. So, before long, our conversation shifted and we were talking about the way things ended with us. I even asked about the day he raped me. He was very apologetic and explained that he had no idea that he had raped me all those years ago. He said he had been drinking heavily that day, and he began to cry and begged for forgiveness. He asked if I would come sit next him on the chaise. At first I said no; but after a while, we were flirting and reminiscing with each other and I went over to where he was sitting. He was looking so intently into my eyes, caressing my ear and the back of my neck and still apologizing for the way things ended between us. He continued on to say how I was still so sweet and beautiful to him. I had not been complimented like that in years, so it felt refreshing to be reminded of my worth as a good woman.

Before I knew it, we were kissing and one thing lead to another and we ended up upstairs. We started out whispering and making small talk and for a split second I thought, *What about Hayden?* Then, all of the horrible things he had done to me over the years came flooding through my mind and those thoughts gave me enough ammunition to ask myself, *What about him?*

Rodney and I had passionate sex that night in the bed I shared with my husband and I enjoyed every moment of it. I felt his muscular body all over me and I just remember thinking, *Man this is nice and feels so much better than the blubber and softness I'm used to feeling with Hayden.* He kissed me so well, he kissed through me. I could not stop. It was riveting and spellbinding. My body was shaking from head to toe. We both enjoyed one another and began to remember being so sensual and passionate together back in 1999 when we were together.

When we finished, we laid in bed talking for a while and then I let him out of the garage door. By then it was almost morning. I refused to go to sleep because I knew I'd have to get right back up in a few hours to get the kids ready and out the door. I took a shower and before long I was lying in bed crying my eyes out. The conviction I felt was enormous! I had never cheated on my husband before, and I felt sick and terribly disgusted with myself. I went over and over in my head about what to do and I cried out to God and apologized.

I got Christian and Miracle off to school and when Braylin, London and I returned home, I called Hayden. I tried not to allow him to hear that I had been crying, but he could tell. When he asked why, I told him my nose was just stopped up. I convinced myself in the wee hours of the morning that I had to tell him, but if so, it needed to be done over the phone because I was too afraid of how he may react.

Hayden started rambling on about the load he had and the big truck. Then I asked him if he had talked to Rodney and he said no. I jokingly said that Rodney and I slept together and he started laughing and said, "Yeah, right. You would never cheat on me; you ain't going nowhere, you stuck with me forever," and he laughed.

At first I kept trying to convince him that I was telling the truth, but when his tone started to change and I could hear the hurt in his voice, I laughed with him and said, "Yeah, I'm just playing."

The pain in his voice for that split second while he was trying to make sure I was just kidding was egregious for me. In all the turmoil he had caused me over the years, it did not bring me joy to hurt him back at that moment. But my deed was already done and I had to confess my sin and get it off my chest. He told me he would be home early that day and we discussed our dinner ideas for that evening before getting off the phone.

Hayden got home at about six o'clock in the evening as I was just finishing up homework time with Christian and Miracle. He came in and went upstairs to take a shower; when he came back downstairs, I told him I needed to talk to him upstairs and I instructed the children to stay downstairs and play. When we got to our room, I closed the double doors and he laid down across our bed. I felt so bad seeing him lay there, that I grabbed him by his shoulders and made him sit back up. I put my big girl panties on mentally and came right out and confessed what I had done. He stared at me with a look of shock at first, and then his shock turned into rage. He started crying and throwing things, punching the walls and slamming doors. I was crying, but I was apologizing to him repeatedly. I told him to calm down so he wouldn't scare the children or make them think he was hurting me.

Hayden went into his closet, unfolded the small chair that just happened to be kept in there and sat there for quite some time. I gathered myself and got the children bathed and off to bed. When I return to our room, he was still sitting in the chair rubbing his head with his gun, like he was the star in a *Lifetime Movie* premier. He'd always been very dramatic and unpredictable; I honestly didn't know what to think at this point. It's very difficult to convey one's mindset when in such a deep state of depression. I was so out of touch with reality that I was present enough to be afraid, but didn't know how to respond. He came back into the room to sit on the bed and I had cried so much that I had a pounding headache and my eyes were bloodshot red. I just kept saying, I'm so sorry and he finally hugged me and tried to get me to stop crying. But I guess the more he thought about my betrayal, the angrier he got, so he went back into the closet. *This was one crazy night!*

At this point, I began to get irritated because at least in my first time wronging him, I had been woman enough to own up to my mistake and tell him the truth. It was selfish of me to expect him to just calm down and we move on; but then again, that was the pattern he had set for the things he'd done during our marriage, so why should I expect things to be any different now.

Neither of us knew what to do. He went downstairs and turned on the TV. I went in the bathroom and called Rodney to tell him that Hayden knew that we had sex and his reaction let me know that he was perturbed. He was not upset that I was convicted to tell Hayden what happened; he was angry at the fact that I had told Hayden that he was the one I had cheated on him with.

I sat there on the other end of the line, staring into space thinking, *Are you serious right now?*

"Quee, you could have made up another name! Now how am I going to come over to see my baby girl and he knows what happened between us?"

"I didn't think of that, I just felt terrible about what had happened and I needed to tell him. But let me get off the phone now, I just wanted you to know he knew just in case he calls you."

"Ok, bye, Queebie. Call me if you need me and my homies to come through."

"Ok, bye, Rodney!"

I took my shower and fell asleep in bed watching TV and waiting for Hayden to cool off and come back upstairs so we could talk. But it was getting really late and he was still downstairs. I did not want to bother him, so I turned the TV off as I rolled over and then drifted back off to sleep. At about 2:00 a.m., I heard some loud weeping! Hayden had come into our room and crawled underneath the bed to cry. *I was flabbergasted!* He had done strange things before, but this was very unusual behavior for the big bad wolf, so I was very confused. I had never seen him that way before. First rubbing the gun on his head, now crying underneath the bed! He was acting very erratic. I didn't know what to do and I didn't know if I could trust what he was about to do so I left the room.

I tried going to sleep on the couch in the game room and he followed me in there asking weird questions about the size of Rodney's penis and how the sex felt. He was starting to get enraged and hostile again. I was so uncomfortable with how he was acting, so I decided to leave home. I went to Walmart and parked in the parking lot. I crawled back into the third row of my Explorer and went to sleep. I knew he had to leave for work very early the next morning, so I waited until right after he left and came back home with the children. I took them to school and Hayden called me later that morning. He wanted for us to pray together and he asked me which marriage book I thought we should start reading in order to help get us through what we were going through. I was puzzled! I did not understand the abrupt change in his attitude. I had always wanted to read and explore marriage the way God says it should be with him, but up until then, he had completely refused.

I ran upstairs to look at our books. I was excited for us to try and make things right the way God intended! I search through all of the books we had and suggested a book called, *Healing The Hurt In Your Marriage...Beyond Discouragement, Anger and Resentment to For-*

giveness by Dr. Gary & Barbara Rosberg. It had been on our bookshelf for years. He agreed that it was a good choice and said we were going to start praying together every morning and reading and praying every night.

"We cannot let the devil tear our family apart!" he said. I had a sense of relief in my heart at the chance to finally start things off right in our marriage.

I was avoiding Rodney's calls and attempting to give the new and improved version of Hayden a fair shot. I kept thinking that finally my prayers had been answered; but unfortunately, the mountain of infidelity would be one we would not get over, at least not together anyway.

After about a week, Hayden and I had already stopped reading and praying together. He was calling me out of my name and judging me as if he had no sin of his own. He would curse me out, brag about his lady friends, and then throw a scripture in at the end about Rodney and me being adulterers. Oddly enough, the affair drew Hayden even closer to Rodney; he was still strangely calling him for advice about our marriage.

I was in a whirlwind of confusion; and before long, I found myself giving up and lusting for the muscles I had felt that late, passionate night. Hayden's attitude and my own desires drove me right back into Rodney's presence. First I told Hayden one of my friends was having a bachelorette party at a hotel way out in Frisco, Texas. But Rodney and I had gotten a hotel suite for that Saturday through Monday in Arlington. I called Hayden to tell him that the girls were paying for me to stay an extra night because of all of the stress I'd been under and he was ok with it. But when I called him Monday morning to say I was on my way home and it only took me a good twenty minutes to get there, Hayden hit the roof! He got in my face yelling and saying that Frisco was almost an hour away and asking how did I get home so fast? I told him that I called him after I had already left the hotel, but he was not trying to hear it. He kept insisting that I had been with Rodney. I ignored him, so he called my momma and told her I was out all weekend and had gotten home from Frisco too soon. He was yelling in the phone and acting unstable.. Surprisingly, Momma called the police and told them to make sure he was not going to hurt me. She did that without even knowing how spot on she was for his past behavior. When the police arrived at our house, Hayden was able to assure the police that everything in our home was copacetic and they left without an incident. But the fact that Hayden had called my Momma in the first place was weird because he had never reached out to my family before, nor had I. Especially concerning our marriage. I think that action on his part was just another ploy by him to get more pity and a desperate attempt to sabotage my character in the eyes of others. He wanted the world to know that I had cheated on him.

The way things were going at home brought Rodney and me closer than ever before. We continued sneaking around to see one another almost daily; and after a while, I could not get enough of him. I was addicted; not only to the sex, but also to someone finally making me laugh. I felt alive, beautiful, and important again. The affair got so bad that when I was not home, Hayden would call Rodney to ask him if I was with him. Of course Rodney would say no, but I was usually right next to him in his passenger seat. We had a field day laughing at

Hayden and role playing to mock him once he hung up the phone. I just didn't care anymore!

I had reached the point of finally realizing that Hayden was not all life had to offer me and I did not have to die a slow and miserable mental death. Over the years, I had given him every chance to try and make things right between us and numerous opportunities to wipe the slate clean and to start fresh. But Hayden had frivolously declined every effort and attempt I could muster up to salvage what was left of our marriage. I was tired! For so many years I had lived for him and gave selflessly everything I had in me to give. I even lost my identity in the process and still nothing worked; until now! But it was much too late for Hayden to take Pastor Tatum's advice and straighten up and fly right. He was on a steep country hill with no breaks and going down faster than a bobsled on ice. The volcano had finally erupted! There was no turning back.

My affair with Rodney sadly became the way Hayden finally understood my pain. He told me the night he cried underneath our bed, that every painful emotion he had caused me in eight years of marriage, he experienced in that one night. I was still experiencing a whirlwind of hurt, confusion, and depression; and to add insult to injury, I was also now cold and self-fulfilling. I found myself wanting Hayden to truly experience all he had put me through during the course of our marriage.

Miracle invited Rodney to our church one Sunday to watch her sing with the children's choir and I did not oppose. I felt it was justified in the same manner that Hayden had recently invited Candy to visit our church but claimed he didn't know she was coming by. She was an ugly duckling with stacked teeth, but I was cordial and polite despite their inconspicuous history. Rodney was running late getting there, but the children's choir opened up for the adult choir for our morning worship service. Rodney strolled in down the hallway and the long wall of windows, so the entire congregation watched as he went to take a seat in the very back. After Miracle was done singing, she went and sat with him and so did I. I don't know what made me go back there to sit down, but the look on Pastor Tatum's and some of the other members' faces was priceless. It was so quiet you could have heard a pin drop in that large room full of people. Hayden was boiling with anger and it did not help that Rodney, Miracle and I were coincidentally dressed in all black. Toward the end of the service, Rodney had to leave because he had just finished working all night and wanted to get some sleep before his Sunday afternoon basketball game. He, Miracle and I excused ourselves and walked outside to his car. Hayden came following behind us, slamming the glass doors and screaming. It was act three in the movie for him. He loved to make a scene and that time was no different. He came in and out of the building repeatedly yelling and trying to draw as much attention to himself as possible. The attendant at the rec center finally asked him to calm down and was shocked at the evident chemistry between me and Rodney. He knew Rodney from an adult basketball league and asked him if he and I were having an affair because of the way we were laughing, talking and interacting with one another. We both laughed and said of course not. But Hayden was yelling otherwise and he wanted the entire neighborhood to hear him.

He walked up and asked Rodney to leave and Rodney told him he was already leaving and would not be disrespected by him. Hayden apologized to Rodney for making a scene and running up on him, and then he went back inside, gathered the children, and sat down in his truck. Rodney hugged Miracle, pulled away in his car and then the six of us left church as well.

Rodney texted me saying to let him know if Hayden got out of line or put his hands on me and I replied ok. Once we got home, Hayden went bananas. I told him I was not going to entertain him and get into a physical altercation with him and warned him if he touched me I would call the police. My statement made him act worse; he tore through the house, as usual, like the Tasmanian devil. I told him we were going to leave until he cooled down, but he blocked us on the stairs and refused to allow us to leave. He took my keys and hid them among his tools in the garage. Then he snatched my phone out of my hand and threw it into the wall, shattering the screen. I was yelling for him to stop because he was scaring the kids, so he drug me down the stairs. He ripped my shirt and threw me onto the couch and sat all 298 pounds of his fat on top of my body while pinning my arms and legs down. I asked the children to call 911, but he cursed at them and they were afraid to call. I asked him to let me go repeatedly, but he just kept pleading that he wanted to talk. I found it difficult to see how any conversation at the magnitude of his anger could end with civil results. Because of his violent history, I was afraid of what he might do to hurt me in his state of mind. I refused to talk to him because he had already crossed the line by dragging me down the stairs, throwing me around, and cursing at my children. As soon as he got off of me, I ran next door and called the police. When they arrived, Hayden had left to avoid being arrested again and they took pictures of my torn clothes, some minor bruises, and the house being in disarray.

Not long after the police left, Kenya called my phone. I could not believe it still worked after Hayden had thrown it against the wall. She said that Hayden called her and told her about Rodney and everything that transpired and that she was on her way over. I told her there was no need for her to come over and that the police had already left. I hung up the phone appalled that Hayden had reached out to my family again. They were all at Grandmomma San's house as usual on a Sunday after church. It was very obvious that Hayden had called there because he wanted a pity committee at any cost and from whomever he could accomplish it by involving them.

I turned out all of the lights in our house and told the kids to go into my closet and sit down to watch a movie on the portable DVD player. I did not want to be bothered and had not had that rapport with my family in twenty-eight years, for them to all of a sudden be so concerned about the wellbeing of me and my babies. Concern was exactly the opposite of what they had; just as I had suspected! Everything in me was saying not to open the door, but Kenya was so persistent when she arrived, knocking on windows and screaming my name. I did not want to draw more attention from my neighbors, so I finally opened the door, only to find out that she had rallied all of my aunts and a few other people to come into my home and spectate.

As I let them in the house, one by one they began taking turns belittling me. They were all being judgmental, rude, and assuming that what had taken place was all my fault because Hayden was a Minister. The ignorance of the whole ordeal was one thing, but to find out that Hayden fled and was hiding out at Grandmomma San's house was a knife inserted and twisted into my back from him and my family.

How could my own family hide and protect the man who had not only put me through pure hell, but had also put his hands on me for almost the last decade of my life?

The biggest mistake I made was never telling others that he was physically and verbally abusive toward me. So now he was looking like the perfect, young minister that lost his sheep and I looked like his horrible, harlot, wife! But I held on to the fact that only God truly knows all that I endured in the last almost nine years of being married to Hayden. I could not fathom their logic; but they already hated me so much without cause, that there was no logic just hatred and deceitfulness.

My Aunt Sharon said, "I can't believe this so-called happy and perfect family is falling apart!" I just looked at her in disgust as the others laughed.

My family did not come to my aid; they came to gloat and relish in the moment of my despair for the gathering of vicious gossip to take back with them. Not one of them asked if the kids and I were ok or if we needed anything. The refrigerator was almost completely empty, but this so-called weekly church-going group of "Christian women" did not bother to exemplify any love or kindness toward us. They came to pour gasoline, instead of water, on an already out of control fire.

Kenya and Auntie Nachelle kept talking about Rodney, but if they had taken the time over the years to get to know me, they would have known two things: one, it was not about me wanting to be with Rodney: and two, just the act of me agreeing to be with him should have been evaluated considerably as to why that happened. I had stepped outside of myself and was watching my life self-destruct, but I was so out of touch with reality that there was nothing I could do to stop the lava of a massive volcano from flowing. Someone should have been smart enough to say, *wait, this is not you, there has to be something deeply wrong and how can we help you get through this because Rodney is not the answer.* But no one did. As horrible as my marriage was, if someone had prophesied to me in 2008, saying that in the next year I would have an affair with Rodney, I would have thought they were a lunatic and swore that would never happen in a million years! Someone should have taken the time to pray for me and my children; not come through my home raiding like a team of CSI officers. They all finally got into their cars and left after Kenya called Pastor Tatum to come get Hayden's things moved out of the house.

Later that evening when I knew Rodney's game was over, I called him to tell him about the events of the evening and he was highly upset. He just kept apologizing to me for everything that I was going through. He asked if he could come over and I told him no, that the children and I were getting ready for bed. He said to call him if I needed anything and that he would call me the next day.

As soon as we hung up, I heard Hayden coming through the door. He said he had been sitting outside watching the house and wanted to know if we could talk. I told him I did not need any more drama and that he should really just go because I was done. He apologized for throwing me around, hiding my keys, breaking my phone, and even calling my family. He said in hindsight he realized that they did not care anything about us and just wanted something to talk about. My reply to him was, "Duh!" Hayden agreed to leave and said he hoped we could eventually work everything out, but that it was really hard for him because every time he looked at me he saw Rodney too. I told him that I really was not interested in working things out with him and that I wanted to get a divorce and move on with my life.

"I don't believe that's what God wants us to do," he said.

"Oh, now you are listening to God," I said in anger.

He admitted that he had been ignoring God's leading for him to change and do right by me, but that he ignored Him because he was not ready to stop cheating on me. He finally left the house after that. I don't even think I was shocked at his response because I had passed far beyond that point! That day had been one I would never forget.

The following week, Rodney went downtown with me to Legal Aid to file for my divorce. I had researched them online and gathered up all of the required information to receive their assistance. They agreed to take my case for free and also provided me with information on how to get financial assistance for battered women with a Dallas County residence. I made another appointment to speak with one of the representatives at Dallas County, and after staying in an interview with her for three hours while Rodney waited for me outside, she approved my case for financial assistance. I had to provide her with a full run down of the domestic violence and infidelity in my marriage and also all of the details of how my affair with Rodney started in the first place.

Rodney and I went everywhere together and he was at the house almost every day. He thought he was my bodyguard and did not want me to interact with Hayden alone because his behavior had become increasingly strange. . Hayden would sometimes be nice and in the next moment, he would be calling the house repeatedly leaving life-threatening messages and calling me out of my name. But due to the temporary court order, we had to meet him at Walmart or Target to exchange the children on alternating weekends. The children said Hayden was sad and depressed all of the time during their visits and that they spent most of their time with Martha and Yolita.

Rodney ended up finally making Hayden feel the pain that he had constantly put me through over the years for a change. The whole situation gave me a way out of a terrible marriage and I was happy to be out. It was certainly the wrong way to leave; but I don't know how I could have mustered up the strength to do it otherwise before Hayden ended up killing me, or vice versa. I don't think I could have stood anymore turmoil being with him. I had reached my breaking point long before then! Hayden would stalk us and sit outside the house parked across the street; sometimes in his big truck which made it obvious to all of what he was doing.

Detective Knotting, of the Cedar Hill Police, called and asked me to come down to the police station after Hayden finally turned himself in for the incident on July 5th. She told me he had been back at the Tri City Jail in Desoto, but his sister had gone and gotten him out again. The detective wanted me to come by to answer a few questions and

I told her that I had my children with me and she asked me to bring them along. She and I sat and talked for about forty-five minutes and she provided me with some information on receiving assistance from the Cedar Hill Food Pantry for groceries and she even wrote a check to pay my electricity bill for that month, because when Hayden moved out, he immediately stopped his direct deposit. He did not care or even ask if the children needed anything.

After we got back home, Detective Knotting called and said Miracle had apparently been drawing while we were at the police station and she left a letter behind that read, *Dear God. I saw my Daddy hit my Mommy again and she's very sad. I don't think she's going to take him back this time. It makes me sad to see her cry. Amen!*

The detective found it and called me, but I thought they were lying in an effort to make Hayden's charges worse and I was trying to take up for Hayden even then, like an idiot! I guess old habits die hard.

"Miracle was not writing while we were there. I don't know why you're trying to make the case worse than it already is. To my knowledge, the children were all playing with blocks and watching cartoons." I said.

She tried to convince me that it was not their practice to falsify information during an investigation, but I barely listened before we hung up. The next day, I was downstairs doing laundry and found a second copy of the same letter in Miracle's folder she had left on top of the dryer. It appeared as though she had bawled it up previously. I called to apologize to Detective Knotting. I told her that I had no idea that my child was feeling a certain way about seeing me sad all the time behind Hayden, so I found it hard to believe that she would write something like that. Thankfully, she was very understanding and said to call her if I had any other questions regarding Hayden's case and we hung up.

I was not planning to move initially, but since the state was paying for it, I opted to move in Mid-August of 2009. For my own safety and that of the children, I also decided not to tell Hayden where we were moving to. The move was bittersweet for me because I really did not want to leave my home and I knew my children would have to adapt to a much different environment. But God not only blessed me to move into a new place without a job, but to also be able to pay my rent up for the first three months. I knew that even in the depths of that horrifying time in my life that my God would still carry me through.

Martha came by with Pastor Tatum to pick up the children's trampoline and move it into their backyard because I would not have the space for it at our new townhome. She was trying to convince me to take Hayden back and kept taking my things out of the boxes. But I was persistent at killing her with kindness and putting them back into the boxes. She then realized that the situation was way beyond her control. When I mentioned to her that I had been hearing what she'd been telling people about me behind my back, she hurried back to the truck. Not once did she utter a word of concern about what I said or any words of encouragement about my situation. Instead, she just quickly tried to change the subject and said she wanted to go with me to a sale the following week. I remember thinking to myself, *you just confirmed that what I have been hearing all this time is true and do you hear yourself right now?*

After several meetings with our lawyers for mediation, we each received a letter to appear in court to address my protective order against Hayden. The purpose of the hearing was to address all of the physical, mental and verbal abuse I had endured from Hayden during our marriage. I begged Hayden not to take our past to court. I told him to just sign the protective order and we could keep his and his family's business out of the street; but no! He had Yolita hire lawyers to fight against something he knew he was guilty of, and he brought the whole church to court with him as character references for his sake. .

The whole situation was so funny to me because the only part of his character that he had allowed them to see was counterfeit! I had been an active member at that church for eight years and an unpaid secretary for four years. My children and I were struggling, hungry, you name it…and the only people from our church that helped us were Brother and Sister Fuller. No one else came and helped us move out of that house or called to see if we needed anything. No one in his family had contacted me and the kids, I had to call them. Mariah came by one day right before we moved out and I cried and still wanted some encouragement from her just from one woman to another. But she was loyal to her little brother; and being his sister, sitting down to talk to me for a few moments just to get a better understanding seemed like a cardinal sin to her.

This whole divorce ordeal was jaw dropping; but what took the cake was my very own biological father, Alvin, asking to address the court on Hayden's behalf. When he approached the stand proud and eager, my eyes were filled with pain and dismay. Long story short, my attorney asked him if he had any knowledge of Hayden being physically abusive toward me. He answered that he hadn't and insinuated that I was probably lying based on his experience of being previously married to my mother over twenty-seven years ago. My lawyer told him his marriage to Momma had absolutely nothing to do with my marriage to Hayden and then she asked him if he and I were close, to which he also answered no.

She slam dunked Daddy when she replied, "Then why in the world would you want to volunteer to testify against your very own daughter and you have no earthly idea what transpired in their marriage?"

He never answered the question, but replied that I was close to my step father Randall, but that he and I had never had a relationship.

My lawyer asked him a series of questions to which he had no factual answers, which left him feeling humiliated and publicly embarrassed. As she dismissed him from the witness stand, he left quickly, slamming the doors of the courtroom. All I could say was "WOW!"

Hayden was then asked to get on the stand and speak about the events of his physical abuse toward me during the course of our marriage. My lawyer had him so cornered with his own lies that he began to stutter and sweat. As he told lie after lie, he quickly found it hard to remember the stories he was making up as he was going along. She was basically asking him the same questions over and over; wording them in a different way, and he could not keep up with the version of the story he'd previously given.

What no one in that courtroom knew – because – Hayden had gotten up there and lied so much, was that his Momma and Daddy had witnessed him hitting me twice before. The first time was when we were living with them and it was late one night. His Dad heard me screaming and ran into the room and his Momma was trying to keep me and the kids from leaving! At the time, they acted as if his abuse was normal behavior in a marriage and that I should just deal with it and stay with him. The second time they witnessed him physically abusing me was when the police came to their house one Sunday afternoon on Mother's Day. Since Hayden's lawyer knew his parents had witnessed both of those incidents, she advised Hayden's parents to wait outside during the hearing. She did that so that his parents could not be called to the stand, but also to prevent Pastor Tatum from having to testify about his physical abuse toward Martha. The apple does not fall far from the tree and Hayden had done so many obscene and disrespectful things all throughout our relationship that there was no reason to wonder why things ended up like they had.

After the court hearing ended in my favor, there was an older, Caucasian bailiff who approached me to ask if Alvin was my real dad. When I replied that he was, the gentleman was appalled. He said he had never seen anything like that before and that it was obvious Hayden was lying.

"Why on earth would your Dad take his side and not protect you?" the man asked.

I had no real answer to that question. All I could tell him was that I had been trying to figure out the same thing. I couldn't understand why, not only had Daddy, but even Alvin Jr. and my uncles had done nothing to defend me. Yet, they had all rallied on Hayden's side just like Momma and her family.

Shortly after the court hearing ended, Rodney and one of Miracle's older sisters, Karinda, moved in with us. I believe that had it not been for Rodney being around the children and I so much, there's no telling what Hayden would have done to stop me from divorcing him. I had the electricity at the house turned off once we started moving, not knowing it was going to take so long to get everything out. In the heat of the summer, disconnecting the lights too early was the wrong thing to do. It took me quite a while to move all of the items from our huge house into a two bedroom townhome, but we did it one day and one load at a time in my Explorer. I remember getting so sweaty, frustrated and burnt out. I had even become angry with God still trying to process why things had ended up this way between Hayden and me after I had been crying out to Him and prayed for us for so many years. I had given that man one hundred percent of myself up until that point; and yet it took all of the prior drama to unfold in order for him to finally realize what he had in me as a wife. Hayden had the audacity to tell me several times in the past, that I would never cheat on him so he did not have to impress me because I would never leave him! But once he realized the house was really empty, he had a brand new outlook.

He called me one day pleading and said, "Nikki, can I please talk to you? I have to get this off of my chest."

"What's up?" I said.

"Nikki, I know you were the one holding our marriage together. I admit it...I kept doing things to make it look like I was cheating on you; from going to the strip clubs while you were thinking I was at work to the hot pink condom in my truck, smoking blacks to experiment, my secret bank accounts, gambling, the women I kept as friends secretly and right down to the naked pictures in my phone. I get it now! I will move away...anywhere you want to go, but please...I just want my family back! I know you had never cheated on me before this year and I told people that you had been cheating on me all along out of anger and spite. I never stood up for you when my momma would always get out of line and be rude trying to loud talk you in front everyone after she would beg us to come over for dinner." He also said, for a lack of better words; forget my momma and the church. I'll leave the church for you. I just want my wife back with me. Please, Nikki! I promise I won't mistreat Miracle anymore. I'll even change jobs if you will just come back. You don't want to be with Rodney after all he's done to you. He's no good and you know it; you're just not thinking straight right now! God has shown me that I'm going to get my family back; but if you don't come back to me, you're going to die. Nikki, God is going to allow something tragic to happen to you because of your disobedience."

I was blown away at Hayden's unmitigated gall as I sat there listening to him admit what he should have done so many years ago. I finally responded to him by saying that if that were the case, God would have taken him out a long time ago for his disobedience!

"Had I known retaliating against you by cheating on you back and admitting it publicly would get this result from you, I would have done it a long time ago! I admit it was wrong to lie and cheat on you and cause all of this turmoil; and for that, I do apologize! But if you really ever loved me, it should not have taken all of this for you to finally realize all of your wrongs and that you have always put your family, friends and job before our marriage and our children. When I was crying out to you for the sake of our marriage, I had even made a list of the times your momma had both physically and verbally harmed me and you did not cover me nor address her. It was starting to make me sick watching you get up and preach and then coming home acting like a totally different person. Hayden, you took full advantage of the kids and I being in your life for as long as I could allow you to, and you also allowed people to mistreat me because you were not man enough to stand up to them. So, in having to stand up for myself, it made me look like the bad, disrespectful daughter-in-law and an un-submissive wife. I always had your back and you know it! I got so lost and tangled up in your world that I had given up on me. I cannot continue to live my life in your shadow while you belittle and disrespect me. I have to go now, it's time for the children to get off of the school bus and Rodney will be home soon!"

He started yelling and cursing me out. I hung up the phone before he could finish his next pathetic statement. Knowing how bipolar he was, I was sure that anything that came out of his mouth at that point was going to be something completely opposite to the conversation we had just had because he could never accept me telling him no.

After a short while, the children became acclimated to Rodney's presence. He and I sat them down and asked what their feelings were about the move and the big changes.

Miracle replied, "Mommy, I'm happy you're not with him anymore because he would always make you sad and hit you and you're not fun to play with when you're sad. I like that you laugh and smile more now."

Then Christian replied, "I'm glad we moved here because life was so much harder over there with Daddy."

I just broke down and started crying because as a parent, you think that your children don't know what's going on, but they are well aware and have their own opinions and concerns. I'm just glad my kids are happy now. I needed to leave Hayden; not just for me, but also for them. I don't wish what I went through on anyone though. I had no idea what was going to come out of all of the chaos, but to God be all of the glory; however, I did know that He would never leave me nor forsake me!

Rodney made me laugh a lot and we played like two elementary school children and just enjoyed being in the company of each other. I could not remember a time when I had been so comfortable just enjoying life and not living in constant pain and tumultuous drama. I had been cooped up for so many years; I was ready to see if I had been missing anything. I had not listened to anything other than Gospel music for years by my own choice. But I didn't know any of the latest songs or dances. On the weekends when my kids were with Hayden and Karinda was visiting her grandmother, Rodney and I would go out. He worked nights at a club in Arlington and had connections at other places in DFW, so every time we went out, we would be in the VIP section.

One night Scarface tried to hit on me at a club in Ft. Worth and I didn't even recognize him until Rodney and his friend told me who he was. It was so funny how out of touch I was. I was only twenty-nine and I felt sixty-nine and way out of my element. But I was starting to get my sanity back and happy to be free and smiling often. I was able to vent a great deal of my frustrations to Rodney and cry through the pain. Aside from the sex and the entire adulterous nature of our current living situation, the moving experience was very therapeutic for me. Thankfully, the good definitely outweighed the bad. I could finally grasp a glimpse of hope for the first time in a very long time. Laughter really does have healing power. The rollercoaster ride that was my life was just about to get a little more interesting.

I guess Alvin was feeling guilty about going to court and making himself look stupid, so he asked if he could come by to visit. Rodney was still angry and didn't understand why I would agree to let him come over after what he'd done in court. When Alvin came by, Rodney went upstairs because he did not want anything to do with my daddy. . I really didn't have much for words where he was concerned either, but I wanted to see if he was remorseful because his actions had proven to me that he never cared anything about my well-being or loved me as his daughter. But of course, he was not at all apologetic! You would think since he and Carissa had also recently separated, he would have been able to empathize more because of the way she had done him. She married him, spent all of his money on clothes, furniture and trips around America, then burnt off with it all. He was pretty down in the dumps. However, he was fifteen years older than her and I could tell she was a no good, lose, psychotic squirrel when Daddy introduced me to her. She had a very jealous spirit; always giving negative and unsolicited advice. She told me once that because I kept such a neat appearance, I would eventually make my children feel inferior.

To which I replied, "That makes absolutely no sense; there's nothing wrong with me teaching them to care about their hygiene and the way they carry themselves. We don't go out in public wearing head scarves, house shoes and pajamas and that's not a crime; especially if I don't want them to end up being ratchet like you."

She laughed, but I was so serious. I did not like her at all and I only tolerated her only for Daddy's sake to keep the peace.

Miracle, Christian, Braylin, and London returned home from being with Hayden while Daddy was visiting. They told him and me that they had spent the night at Carissa's along with Hayden and heard her calling Hayden baby. Daddy ignored their comments and quickly changed the subject. I saw that Daddy obviously did not want to believe what they were saying, so I waited until he left to call Hayden. I wanted to hear from the horse's mouth why my children would need to witness such disgusting behavior and to know exactly what happened.

Why on earth would my children, and soon-to-be ex-husband, be sleeping over at my soon-to-be ex-step-mother's apartment?

When Hayden answered the phone, he admitted that they had all spent the night over there more than once, but it was innocent. I knew he was lying about the innocent part because he kept putting way too much emphasis on it; plus, I know him all too well. He said that Carissa wanted the children to come visit and he always slept on the couch when they went to spend the night. Rodney and I had a great time laughing at that pathetic situation. *Gross!* How desperate could two people be? Especially since Daddy just testified on Hayden's behalf and he still attends Pastor Tatum's church to this day.

Surprisingly, Teresa also stopped by that same day. This was out of the norm for her to want to spend time with me, so I didn't really know what to think of it. But I had always wanted the moral support of my sisters. Honestly, I was not sure if she was really checking on me or if she was spying for Momma. I was just glad she didn't really want to discuss the whole Hayden fiasco, other than mentioning he had been calling her, Momma, Kenya, and several other people on both sides of my family almost every day to talk about me.

People were so foolish to listen to one side of a story and not the other, saying that I had lost my mind. Rumors were flying left and right; and both sides of my family had rallied to Hayden's defense, so I never knew who to trust. He had been calling them individually, giving his sob story and begging for pity. Even some of my friends had run into him out at grocery stores and gas stations and said he wanted pity from them as well. He was giving everyone the same rehearsed speech over and over again. Hayden was also in contact with Momma and Randall, and Momma seemed to be eating all of this foolishness up by being happy to oblige Hayden and entertain his lies. I got so tired of trying to explain things to her and everyone else, that I started lying to protect myself because they were just using everything I said against me and creating more rumors, but pretending to be concerned and wanting to help.

I had also tried reaching out and asked Kenya if my nieces could come over to play with Miracle and she replied, "Absolutely not! I don't agree with the lifestyle you're living."

As if she was without spot or wrinkle as the secretary and school director at her church. She was so hypocritical that she did not even care about how much that hurt me, let alone, all I was going through.

Grandmomma Emily was the only one that did not judge me and she was concerned about us. She asked why I had not told anyone about Hayden abusing me and just expressed her unconditional love toward me.

Teresa seemed to be positive and mostly wanted to discuss Miracle and me being a part of her upcoming wedding. I told her I would be happy for us to participate and asked if Rodney could escort me to the event, and she said yes. I did appreciate the gesture of kindness and her taking the time to come by. I was very grateful for her support and excited to see how happy she was to be getting married to Lawrence Tyler, the father of her two daughters. He was a very nice guy and kind of puts you in the mind frame of the actor, Columbus Short. He and Teresa went to Town View High School and to Texas A&M Commerce University together.

A few weeks after Teresa's visit, Momma called. She was ready for me to come over to go grocery shopping with her. At the time, I was able to bless her and Randall with about $200 worth of groceries every month because they were having a hard time financially. I didn't mind because God had been such a blessing to my children and I, and He had provided for our every need throughout the entire devastating storm in our lives.

When I went by Momma's house, she waited until we arrived at the grocery store to inform me that she would be using my contribution for her household toward food for Teresa's wedding instead. I was bothered by that because it came off to me as manipulative. I didn't mind helping with the food for my little sister's wedding at all, but the way Momma went about it was shady to me. What she failed to realize was that had she been honest, I would have been more than happy to help with food for the wedding and her household groceries. I even offered to get her and Randall's things as well, but she declined.

When Teresa's wedding day arrived, I had my red bridesmaid's dress ready to go. Rodney, Miracle and I were dressed to perfection and ready to have some fun. I was very excited for Teresa and Lawrence and looking forward to celebrating with them. However, by that time, both sides of my entire family were rooting for Hayden and revved up by his many lies and sob stories, so I was unsure of what events the night would unveil. I was prepared to avoid any potential drama that surfaced. I had not seen my family for quite some time, but I had heard about the rumors they were spreading about me and my marriage.

When I saw them at the wedding, I attempted to avoid them completely. I've never been a huge fan of smiling and being fake by holding a conversation with people who I know have been talking about me like a dog. Well, of course, my ignoring them was not going to fly with Aunt Sharon. As we were leaving the church headed to the venue for their reception, she followed me all the way down the hall inside New Birth Baptist Church and out to my truck; talking trash as usual.

She was offended because I did not bother introducing Rodney to any of them. My reply to her was, "Why would I do that and y'all have been talking badly about him and me for the past few months?"

She was on fire. I thought she was going to faint because she was obviously very appalled by my response.

She then yelled out, "You never called me for help!"

"That is not true, and don't pretend as if you had no idea what was going on. Ya'll were all so excited to come out to my house at Hayden's request when all of this began, and you were the main one gloating at the time! I have a phone too, and I-35 runs both ways. I am the one in distress and if my so-called family cared about me, they all should have reached out to me."

I told Miracle to get in the truck; she and Rodney where looking puzzled and scared.

Aunt Sharon then tried scolding me by saying, "You don't walk off while I'm talking to you."

Of course, I kept walking as she continued following me to my truck. I opened the passenger side door and reached into the glove compartment to get my wallet out and she stopped yelling in mid-sentence and hurried off to her car. Rodney and I fell out laughing. He said she must have thought I had a weapon in the glove compartment or something. We drove to the reception, talking and happy that the moment of drama had passed. When we arrived, we were able take a few pictures and get something to eat. After we finished eating, I asked Rodney if he was ready to go change into some casual clothes to dance. So we walked out to the truck to get our change of clothes, and lo and behold, Hayden of all people was sitting outside in his truck. I was livid! I asked him what in the world was he doing at my sister's wedding reception. He said Randall and Momma called and asked to borrow his truck to help them haul some things for Teresa's wedding. Apparently, the truck would not start and Randall had to call him to come pick it up. I could not help but feel betrayed. I wondered why on earth, out of all the people in the world, they would still want to deal with Hayden; especially at the height of such a huge storm between him and me. It also hurt me because I couldn't understand why they didn't care about what he had put me through. But in hindsight, I don't think Momma and Randall borrowed his truck to hurt me, but that they just needed help and they were so used to Hayden being reliable in a crunch.

Rodney begged me not to call the police, but I did anyway. I wanted them to enforce the restraining order that was in place for Hayden. When they arrived, most of my family was out on the sidewalk siding with Hayden. The police said that they could not enforce the restraining order because he did not go inside the building. I asked them why was it necessary for someone to have a restraining order, if when it's violated, nothing happens. I was so upset and unsure of what would happen after the police left that the three of us went home.

I cried aloud and vented to Rodney because I was so hurt and could not understand why my family would continuously support someone who had been vastly abusive toward me for the last decade. They have no earthly idea what I endured in my marriage with Hayden and yet, when they were made aware of it, none of them cared. They upheld him as if he was completely faultless and I was the villain. I was so undone! The only reason I regret calling the police that night, other than the fact that they were completely useless, was that I missed out on the rest of my sister's reception. I wish I could've celebrated her that evening, but I was totally caught off guard and unaware that the enemy would be infiltrating in the night.

I apologized to Teresa and Lawrence a few weeks after things had time to cool down, but I couldn't wrap my head around what to do with my feelings toward Momma, Randall and my other family who'd failed at being there to support me during the worst storm of my life.

It was finally the end of December 2009, and I was looking forward to celebrating a new year with a fresh start. However, I had no idea what that would entail. I had been frequently reading my Bible and crying out to God in my small bedroom closet, looking for direction and peace. The confusion and drama was taking a toll on me; one minute I was happy to be with Rodney, and the next minute, I felt like I would be better off by myself, getting to know me.

I had even written Rodney a long four-page letter about two months prior, explaining why I thought things could never work between us, but he assured me that I would not feel that way once the weight of my pending divorce was over. I had recently become employed at the AAA call center and had completed my training. On December 31, 2009, my alarm clock went off at 6:00 a.m. and I hit the snooze button. I was so tired, I rolled back over to get a few more minutes of sleep and I heard the audible voice of God as clear as day say to me, "How long are you going to do this?"

I immediately sat up and crawled out of bed, leaving Rodney asleep and went into my closet and wept. I had received some unctions from Him before, but not this precise and direct. That moment was so powerful to me because God was letting me know that as bad as things were in my life, He was still with me. I knew exactly what I needed to do and there was no question that the Lord was calling me out of my current sin-filled living situation.

I went downstairs, and out of all of the people in the world, I called Hayden and told him what God had just said to me. He was extremely excited to find out that I had made up my mind to part ways with Rodney. Unfortunately for him, he also immediately assumed that it meant we should reconcile. Although I was never led to go back to Hayden, I knew I also needed some closure there as well. I felt somewhat obligated to at least explore that notion in order to be absolutely certain. He asked if I would go to the New Years' Eve Watch Night service at Willow Grove Baptist Church with him and the kids and I agreed to meet them there.

I hung up with him and went back upstairs to get dressed for work. When I clocked in at work, my mind was so unsettled that I could not focus on anything except trying to come up with a way to break the news to Rodney. I had to put him out that day. I sat there as long as I could, and finally I told my manager that I had an emergency at my home and needed to leave immediately. I abruptly clocked out and drove all the way home dreading the conversation that was about to take place. Although I was happy at that point in my life, I also realized I was not on the right path for my life.

I called Rodney on my way home and told him we needed to talk and he thought I meant later that night, but I told him I was almost home. He got off the phone, obviously concerned and perplexed at why I needed to leave work so urgently to speak to him. I'm sure he was wondering what must be so important that I would leave for work and return home only an hour later.

I pulled up to the townhouse and sat in the car for a few minutes. I finally mustered up enough courage to get out and go inside. When I walked through the front door, Rodney was so excited to see me; that made what I needed to tell him that much harder to say. He embraced me with his bright smile and strong, muscular arms.

"What's up, Queebie?"

Sadly I became a coward in one and a half seconds. At first, I tried to accuse him of cheating and demanded that he leave immediately. He took that conversation in stride and pretty much blew it off, knowing there had to be another reason for me to be putting him out on New Year's Eve. I began to cry and then I apologized to him and explained what I had heard God speak to me earlier that morning. I assured him that I did care about him and wanted to help him find another place to live, but he definitely had to leave my house that night. He began to cry aloud and Miracle and Karinda were home waiting for their ride with Karinda's grandmother. They began to cry when they overheard him pleading and continuously asking why he had to leave. Thankfully, Christian, Braylin and London were gone with Hayden for Christmas break.

Rodney cried and cried, begging to stay with me for the next fifteen hours. He even had one of his Pastor friends come over to try and talk me out of putting him out. After about thirty minutes of not changing my mind, he left.

At about 8:30 p.m., Rodney finally realized my mind was set and he began loading his belongings into my truck and trying to call around to friends and family to find a place to go. He'd called several people, but was not immediately successful. Finally, he spoke with his sister Towanda and she said he was welcome to stay with her. She wanted us to meet her at her church that night for their Watch Night Service so he could put his clothes in her car and then go to his night job.

I drove him to her church around 10:30 pm and we waited for about thirty minutes, but she was nowhere to be found. We then drove just around the corner because he had another Pastor friend in Desoto. I stayed behind in the truck while he went inside to interrupt their Watch Night Service to ask permission to move in with him and his wife. He finally came back to the truck and said he had to wait for him to come down from the podium, so I was sitting in the truck waiting for almost an hour. Finally, they agreed to allow him to stay with them, so we drove to their house in Grand Prairie, where I helped him un-load all of his things into their garage, using their personal alarm code. Finally I drove him to work at the Bijou Lounge in Arlington. Rod-ney got out of my truck at 11:59 p.m., December 31, 2009. I was so exhausted both physically and emotionally. The night had truly been a spiritual battle. I had absolutely no energy to make it to the church service in South Dallas with Hayden and the kids, so I headed home. Hayden became upset and kept trying to convince me to come so we could hear from God concerning our marriage. He was trying to take me way too fast.

After the fifteen-hour rollercoaster ride that Rodney had just taken me on, I was drained. I was also leery about showing up at that church with him because it was the church that my Momma and sisters attended. I did not want to give everyone the wrong impression that Hayden and I are back together. Plus, Rodney was still texting my phone to check on me, but I would not respond. Hayden called to see if I made it home from Arlington. I told him I had been there long enough to take a shower and climb into bed, but we would have to talk later because I was so tired. I was off of work the next day and grateful for the opportunity to sleep in. Hayden called me that morning asking if he could come over to bring the kids by to see me. I knew that was code for *can we talk,* but I allowed him to come by because I had not seen my babies in two weeks.

He wanted to gain insight on my thoughts concerning our marriage since Rodney had moved out. He and I sat downstairs and talked for hours and nightfall was approaching when he suggested that since neither of us knew for sure if we should stay together, that we should postpone our pending divorce decree. Although I was a bit apprehensive at first for obvious reasons, he did have a valid point. There was still a great deal of uncertainty lingering like a dark cloud over our past and our future. I agreed to call my lawyer to postpone the divorce only if he agreed to make some drastic changes in his attitude and priorities.

A few weeks had passed, and we began some very intense counseling sessions at a local church and even joined an in-home marriage group with some marriage mentors from the same location. I was not very excited about going to counseling; for one, because we had done it together so many times before; and for two, I was warring with my flesh and still entertaining Rodney somewhat. He still wanted to be with me even after finding out I had agreed to make an attempt to reconcile with Hayden. I finally had to tell him once we started counseling that I wanted to give the sessions an honest effort. I had to stop seeing him and without his influences, try to really hear from God. I needed to know if I was doing the right thing or if I was wasting my time again with Hayden.

Rodney was gracious enough to respect my decision and move on. Of course, it did not take him long to find another girlfriend that he could mooch from. He is notorious for finding women, usually in desperate situations, that would not mind taking care of him and buying him a car. As out of it as I was, I would have never done that for him, but this time we could remain friends and keep in touch for Miracle's sake.

Hayden and I went to counseling weekly at Trinity Church in Cedar Hill and it ended up being very helpful for me. Our counselor, Pastor Benny, started out by allowing both of us to lay out our concerns while the other listened. That took up the first two or three sessions because there was so much information to cover.

After evaluating our marital history, Pastor Benny told Hayden that he would like to start by saying, "It takes a very long time for a woman to give up on her marriage or to have an affair." He provided a metaphor that Hayden was not happy with, describing an open field. He said Hayden had left me out in the middle of it, unprotected and opened to being devoured. He also mentioned that none of what had happened was about Rodney. He made it clear that at the point of depression that I had reached, it could have been anyone because Hayden had left the door wide opened by not loving me as Christ loved the church.

He continued by explaining that God held Hayden accountable for me as my husband, and that he had failed to lead and cover our family. Hayden was furious at first, but he could not deny that all of what he was being told was certainly the truth. He told Pastor Benny that he had just written me off as crazy and jealous, so he continued to ignore me crying out to him the entire time we had been married. He said that God had been dealing with him for years concerning me, but he chose to continue to ignore Him and be disobedient because he wanted to keep doing what he was doing. Hayden had become lazy and extremely comfortable in our relationship. He really believed that he could have kept up his terrible behavior and that I would have never retaliated.

Pastor Benny then explained to him that a person can only take so much mistreatment and the more pressure that builds up, the more explosive the end result will be, thus Rodney. Hayden's eyes began to fill with tears and I could tell by his demeanor that the confirmation of that profound revelation hit him like a ton of bricks.

Pastor Benny continued by saying, "This is a spiritual battle and neither of you showed up with the tools and spiritual armor that God has equipped you with to win the fight. Even your children have been left out, because Nikki was depressed and Hayden you checked out of this marriage at its inception! You've allowed your family to control your marriage, while you slept in a fairytale land waiting for all of the work that marriage takes to work itself out without your effort."

The session left me experiencing a combination of emotions because on one hand, I felt like a huge weight had been lifted to hear someone else explain to Hayden the feelings I had been trying years to convey to him and also to witness him finally grasp it and on the other hand, I felt overwhelmed and wounded; wondering how in the world we were going to pull everything back together.

It was as if a huge tornado had come through and demolished our marriage and we had no clue which brick to start rebuilding with and quite honestly, I was not sure if I had the strength to try again. We needed a miracle! In all that we were enduring and learning in counseling, there was a small glimpse of light for us.

It was April of 2010, and we had managed to evict the people who were renting our house out illegally. It was very difficult to get them to leave because when I moved out in August 2009, I had signed the house over to a guy name Greg Baines and he turned out to be a con artist posing as a broker. But once Hayden threatened to sue him, he gave us the warranty deed to our house back. He had convinced a lady named Esperella Aguirre, whom he'd originally rented the house out to, that he was selling her the house for $20,000 cash and she actually paid him and then in turn, rented the house out to another couple who'd just recently moved in a few weeks earlier. It was a huge mess! Her husband divorced her for forking over the $20,000 against his wishes because he knew it had to have been a scam for someone to be willing to sell her a $190,000 home for only $20,000.

At any rate, when we arrived to move our furniture back in the house, it was pouring rain and Esperella had jammed the garage door locked and tried to keep us out. Meanwhile, my furniture was being ruined in the rain. Hayden convinced her children to open the front door and she was livid. We ended up having to call the Cedar Hill police because her tenants had already moved out once we told them their lease was fraudulent, but they returned the keys to Esperella and she was refusing to leave or allow us to bring our things in out of the rain.

The police arrived and we provided them with the warranty deed and closing documents and they told Esperella that she was in the wrong and should leave; but they could not force her to leave because this was a civil matter. She then called her lawyer to come over who ended up helping her see that we were telling her the truth and she did not own any rights to the property. Thankfully, the rain had slacked up and we had some minor water damage to the entertainment center, but that was it. The two-hour unforeseen delay caused us to not finish moving until late that evening. By the grace of God, Pat and Andee Cooper, two amazing friends of ours from the marriage mentor group endured helping us the entire day.

It did not take very long for us to get settled in and completely unpacked, but the environment was stealthy and weird. We spent the first several months trying to turn our focus away from our marriage, and on to working out with Teresa and Lawrence at their house almost every week. We tried clinging to anyone at that point; hoping that after so much time had passed, that the healing and trust would come. That only lasted for so long because the tension was still very surreal in our home. We had not been diligently working on rebuilding our marriage and Hayden was reverting back to his abusive behavior. It was so bad that we ended our counseling sessions because neither of us saw the point of continuing to go if we were still unsure about being together.

I especially no longer wished to spin my wheels in counseling when my heart and mind were made up to be done with him for good. We were not romantically involved and even a slight attempt would result in an argument.

Our communication was defective and ambiguous because neither of us trusted the other person and rightfully so. I even started sleeping in Miracle's room with a chair wedged underneath the doorknob because I was not sure what Hayden's mindset was. He would be kind and understanding one minute, and unpredictable and irate the next. The threat of uncertainty day in and day out was becoming very frightful and depressing. I refused to go into another mental tailspin with that man. I had given him enough of myself mentally and in every other way possible.

I decided to enroll at Mountain View College while working full time in order to be away from him as much as possible. Being around him was very challenging because he would continuously inquire about my sexual encounters with Rodney. It had been over a year since my affair and all he ever wanted to talk about anymore was Rodney. Quite frankly, I was quickly growing tired of him asking questions and judging me, so I became brutally honest. Hayden was very irrational. He was so broken, but all I could think about was all of the pain he had subjected me to in the past and how he never provided any compassion toward me while I was on the receiving end. In that moment, my heart was merciful toward him, yet still cautious and nonchalant.

I had always loved Hayden and never wanted our marriage to reach such a low point. I would have never imagined the day would come where I had lost all hope, because I always had hope that things between us would finally change and we would make it with a huge testimony and maybe even our own marriage ministry. But by the time we were trying to make things better at the final attempt, I no longer cared about holding on to that hope or what the end result would be between us.

Hayden could tell that my patience had grown very thin with saving our marriage. We were approaching the end of 2010 by then, and the pressure of the relationship was equivalent to a swelling pipe on the cusp of bursting. The whole ordeal compelled him to divulge most of the ugly truth of every questionable moment he had previously been involved in over the course of our entire marriage, starting with the events of 2001. He asked me to take a seat with him on my closet floor so the children could not hear what he was about to say. In his pleading to convince me not to divorce him, he confessed that he was in the strip club in a private room getting a lap dance and the girl asked him for sex and gave him the hot pink condom. He then went to the bathroom to put it on and thought of me and ran out of the club still wearing it. He said that when he got inside his truck, he took it off and put it inside the paper cup and had forgotten about it. He explained that all of the women he had entertained over the years were never serious offenses, but that he allowed the chaos because he was bored.

I don't know how long we sat in my closet, while Hayden allowed me to ask him about every incident that I could possibly think of and he provided the answers like word vomit. But I was not quite prepared for the answer he had to my very last question.

I began the question by explaining to him that Miracle and Christian had mentioned that they had heard Carissa, Daddy's jezebel of a wife, calling him baby during their sleepover at her house with him. At first, Hayden became extremely quiet and cautious about his response. He then paused and stated that he wanted very badly for us to start fresh, so he was willing to come clean and lay everything out on the table.

He took a deep breath and blurted out, "Yes, I did have unprotected sex with Carissa several times. But that's no different than you being with Rodney; he's a man and she's just a woman."

Surprisingly, I was not angry, but literally sick to my stomach at the audacity of them both. I could not help but think, *it could have been anyone, why her?* Daddy had told us how gross she was with the men in her past, why would Hayden knowingly open himself up to sexually transmitted diseases? Then I was disgusted at the thought of ever having sex with Hayden again after he'd had intercourse with someone my father had sex with. That admission was way too much for me and there were certainly no more thoughts of reconciliation on my part. My psyche would not allow me to dismiss that fact and I was having flashbacks about A.B. Had I known a year ago that he and Carissa had actually been sexually involved, I would have never made an attempt to reconcile with Hayden. I think that's why he decided not to reveal it during our counseling sessions. Plus, it made me wonder if Hayden and Carissa had been sexually involved prior to our separation in 2009, when I first saw Rodney.

Hayden could tell how apprehensive and tense I was to respond to him initially. I think he was expecting to unload all of the weight he had been carrying around on his shoulders for so many years and magical fairy dust was going to instantly heal my heart towards him and entice me to leap into his arms.

When he got the extreme opposite reaction from me, he went on a one-man rampage, proceeding with the usual punching of holes in the walls and tearing through the house like a human tornado. He was screaming and yelling obscenities to the children and me. Saying to them, "Carissa was only a woman and me sleeping with her is no different than Mommy sleeping with Rodney."

At first he would not allow me to leave the room so they were visibly shaken by all of the commotion and following him through the house trying to reason with him. I decided if I could find a way to remove myself from the situation maybe he would calm down because Grandmomma Emily always said, "It takes two fools to keep an argument going!"

As soon as he turned his back, I grabbed the house phone and ran to lock myself in the master bathroom to get away from him. That made him angrier because he was determined to change my mind and make me hear him out. I told him I was done arguing and so not in the mood for one of his usual temper tantrums. I never understood why he thought his violent temper would make me want to hear him out.

He stood in the hallway of the master suite yelling for me to unlock the door, but I refused. I begged him to stop and to please calm down because he was scaring the kids. I could hear them crying on the other side of the door, but he continued and then began punching holes into the door so hard that he came completely through the door like the Incredible Hulk, leaving only the bottom half of it hanging on the hinges. There were wood and paint chips all over the bathroom floor. The children were standing behind him screaming and terrified at what he might do next. I immediately dialed his parents' home phone number to avoid him getting arrested, yet again, for being stupid. Martha answered the phone and I frantically requested for them to please come and get their son before I had to call the Cedar Hill police on him.

She sarcastically replied, "What have you done now?"

I went platinum plus. "I haven't done anything to your son, but it would be in your best interest to come calm him down."

I guess she could sense the anger in my voice, so she passed the phone to Pastor Tatum. To my amazement, he already knew what the problem was. He didn't even give me an opportunity to go into the details of what was transpiring because he said God had already shown him that Hayden and Carissa were sexually involved and he knew once I found out that I would not be okay with it or want to be with Hayden anymore. He said he was hoping we would be able to work things out, but once that was revealed to him, he was not sure anymore how things would go. He further explained that he tried to tell Martha what God had said and she refused to believe him.

Hayden knew I was seriously done with him when I took the initiative to call his parents' myself, because whenever we fought, I never wanted him to call them for fear of them being bias and upholding him in his wrongdoing. I confirmed that Pastor Tatum was on his way, then I hung up the phone and Hayden asked me one last time, "Nikki, are you sure we can't work this out? After I leave this time, I am not coming back," his demeanor came off as if he was doing me some sort of favor by staying.

I happily replied, "Let's be very clear, I have absolutely no desire to be with you. I am not attracted to you and I finally realize that you never really loved me. You have wasted so many years of my life living a lie. I am certainly done with you, Hayden Tatum! I'll go back downtown to refile the divorce decree first thing on Monday morning."

He gave his usual smug look and shrugged his shoulders, got up and began packing his things. I was so relieved that he went to pack without first hitting or shouting or punching a wall, but I think he acted that way only because he knew his Dad was on his way over.

Pastor Tatum arrived quickly and helped Hayden move all of his things back into their home. I had no convictions from the Lord and no more reservations about cutting ties with that man. I was finally at peace with not sharing the rest of my life with him. For the first time in a very long time, I could see the light of day and I felt so hopeful for the future of my children and for me. All I could do was pray that God would keep us and that someday they would understand why I could not stay married to Hayden.

Miracle and Christian were eleven and nine at the time, so I was more concerned about their ability to understand things, than I was about Braylin and London because they were only five and three at the time. My children had witnessed that man terrorize me for years. But thanks be to God they came through the fire of the explosive relationship unharmed.

CHAPTER ELEVEN

Jesus was there all along!

As soon as Monday morning arrived, I high tailed it back down to the Legal Aid office before dawn that cold January morning in 2011. I had a lawn chair in my truck that I placed at the door of their office at 5:00 a.m., to wait for them to open at 8:00 a.m. From the previous filing, I knew they would only accept the first thirty applications that they received each day, so I was determined to be the first in line.

It was a little eerie being downtown outside in the dark; but I was a woman of determination, on a long, overdue mission to freedom and peace! When they finally opened three hours later, there was a trail of people lined up around the building behind me. Thankfully, because we had previously filed, it was easy for them to resume our request to divorce, so sitting outside freezing my toes off was well worth the wait.

Throughout the entire process of the divorce, I had tunnel vision. My schedule was saturated with work, school, and taking care of my babies. I was very proud of the strides I was making in college seeing as how I had graduated from high school over a decade ago. I enrolled in a Spanish folklore dance class and the history of dance. I met a very dear friend in that class named Angel Coleman-Harris. We hit it off instantly and have still maintained an awesome friendship all these years later. God always knows when we could use a good friend. She and I have very similar testimonies and marital experiences. She was already divorced and happily engaged to her Prince Charming, Brent. They were so good together. Little did I know, my happiness was not very far behind; but first, I had to learn more about myself and who was not meant to be a part of my life.

My divorce was finally finalized in April, 2011, and I was a little reluctant to start dating. To be quite honest, I had never had the opportunity to date much before, and the thought of it was like learning how to tie my shoes all over again. It was hilarious! I was going out with Monique as frequently as our busy schedules would allow while the children were visiting Hayden at his parents' house. I really enjoyed hanging out with Monique, but it didn't take long for me to realize that the nightclub scene was not for me. It had not changed one bit and I never wanted to get involved in a serious relationship with someone there.

I was taking my time and trying to focus on school. But everyone was trying to hook me up! My sister-in-law Sondra introduced me to her cousin, Tony Daniels. It was weird that I had never met him before, especially considering the fact that Sondra and Alvin Jr. had been together for almost seventeen years. Tony worked as a postal clerk at the main post office in Dallas. Sondra gave him my number, and when he called, we hit it off really well. We talked on the phone for two weeks before we actually met and went out on our first date. Just talking to him over the phone, he seemed like a really nice guy and looked quite handsome wearing a hat in the pictures I had seen of him.

He asked me what I liked to do and I told him I was still a kid at heart and liked to do pretty much anything that was fun. I was very excited to finally be meeting him in person, but also super nervous. I had gotten my stylist to do my hair and arch my eyebrows. I went to the nail salon and I picked out an outfit from my closet that was still fairly new. I really didn't know what to expect because he told me it would be a surprise, so I wasn't sure how I should dress. I was dolled up, but somewhat casual chic.

Tony arrived at exactly 7:30 p.m. as he'd promised. When he rang the doorbell, I could have fainted, I had not been that nervous in years. I opened the door and we greeted one another with a friendly hug. I kind of looked him up side his head because I wasn't expecting him to be the same height as me, which made him shorter than me when I wore heels. Dating someone his height was a first for me. I guess looking at his pictures, I couldn't really tell how tall he was because he was sitting down. He was not as handsome as in his pictures either, but he wasn't the worst I had seen and he had an awesome personality. He seemed pretty nervous too, but I was very impressed with his chivalry. He open doors for me, stood until I sat down at dinner and was polite and very funny.

The first stop on our date was Mimi's Café in the Highlands of Arlington. It was okay, but neither of us enjoyed the food enough to want to go back. We left there and went to Dave and Buster's and Splitzville. We had such a wonderful time that afterwards, we decided to walk over to Studio Movie Grill, but it had gotten so late that there were no more movies playing that night. We decided to walk down to Charmin Charlie's where we sat on a bench, underneath the stars, facing the store window. We sat there talking for an hour or more. We were really enjoying one another's company. It was so crazy how we had grown up in the same neighborhoods and knew a lot of the same people, but had never met before that night. We were having such a great time together, that during our date, we decided to go to Six Flags the next day.

By the time we made it back to my house it was already after 1:00 a.m. and we sat on the couch watching TV and talking until like 2:30 a.m. in the morning. He asked if I'd mind if he spent the night seeing as though we were going to Six Flags first thing in the morning. I reluctantly said yes, but only because I knew my family knew him and I had given Monique his name, phone number, and date of birth before our date.

I could tell by his Casanova demeanor, that Tony was certain he would get the opportunity to sleep with me that night. So when we reached the top of the stairs, I directed him down the hall. I could tell that he was completely dumbfounded. He said he had never been told no before concerning sex and I laughed and told him that was sad and we said good night! I slept with my bedroom doors locked that night, but he never tried anything sneaky.

As a matter of fact, it took quite some time before we became physical. I had been reading Steve Harvey's book on relationships and the ninety-day rule. We were spending almost every day together, but I would not waiver in my decision. Tony was definitely rudely awakened. I took my time because I was still trying to get to know him as a person. He was very patient the whole time; but as soon as I finally let my guard down, I began to notice several red flags and character flaws. *What I like to call a person's true colors!* I honestly think he was battling with something more spiritual than physical. However, he started showing signs of unreliability and dishonesty. Several stories and instances were beginning not to add up. I have a very vivid and precise memory and he would forget the story or excuse he had given me for not coming over the day before by the next time I actually saw him.

Another concern I had was that he never wanted me and his youngest son's mother to meet or speak over the phone nor on Facebook. But he wanted me to believe that they were just friends now and that he helped her out, from time to time, by giving her a ride home from Walmart at midnight. She worked the evening shift there, part time. Grandmomma Emily had cautioned me that because their son was still very young, there was a great possibility that they were still sexually involved. I was having Hayden flashbacks and praying and contemplating on how to break it to Tony that I didn't want to be with him anymore. My only regret was that I didn't wait just a little longer to begin opening my heart up to him.

After I confronted Tony with the inconsistencies in his stories, he explained them away as miscommunications. We enjoyed the rest of our evening together, but I still had several question marks in the back of my mind, so I was still praying for guidance. He went to church with me that Sunday, and as we were leaving, a lady gently approached me and began to prophecy over my life.

She said, "Hi, I know you don't know me from Adam, but I wanted to be obedient to the Spirit of the Lord. God has seen you and your children suffering. I don't know the pain you recently endured, but God told me to tell you that He's going to send you a man that will love you past all of your hurt. He's going to be a peaceful breath of fresh air to you and your children and he's going to love them as his own. Just hang in there, your blessing is coming!"

I wept and fell into her arms thanking God because I knew she had to have been sent to me by Him. How else would a stranger know I have children and had recently gone through a whirlwind of a terrible marriage? Tony was standing there looking very lost and confused.

When we got into the car he said, "I guess that lady wasn't describing me because she said God is going to send you a man."

I had no reply for him, but my thoughts were very much so in agreement with what he was feeling. I certainly knew then that I needed to break up with him, but I needed to stop being so nice and figure out a way to say it. I realized something about myself in that moment. I can be a little too nice to people and that's why they mistake my kindness for weakness. But there's absolutely no nice way to say, *I'm done with you!*

Tony had been very supportive financially and fun to hang out with, but something just did not sit well within my spirit concerning him. After the prophecy, I began distancing myself from him by not answering the phone or texting him as much as I used to, and when he'd come to visit, he noticed that my demeanor was cold. Finally he asked me why it felt like goodbye between us. I just smiled at him and gave him long hug. Finally, the push of courage I needed came full speed ahead.

He was outside getting something out of his car and I was upstairs sitting on my bed, watching television and his phone began to chirp aloud while lying next to me. I picked it up to take it to him and saw the heading of a very explicit text from a girl named Nicole. He had previously introduced me to this person at his mother's house as a longtime friend of their family. Forgive me, but this girl looked like the long lost twin of Sammy Davis Jr., so I was very offended that he would completely downgrade. When I got downstairs, I calmly handed him the phone and waited to see what his reaction to the text would be. That joker was stuttering and lying like a rug. I can't say that I was hurt because God had already confirmed that we were not meant to be together, but I was angry with him for all the lies he had told and angry at myself for believing him.

He went outside and thinking he had deleted every text message and emptied his call log, he came back inside to hand me his phone. I told him that there was still one text he forgot to delete from Nicole asking him when he was coming back over there... apparently he had been at her place just a few nights prior. He then dived across the bed laughing and wrestling the phone out of my hand and trying to come up with an explanation. I warned him when we first started dating that I had a very low tolerance for games and I did not have the strength or the capacity to settle again in a relationship. He got angry and left and I politely shut the door behind him and went upstairs to bed. He called my phone all that Thursday night and all day on Friday, but I would not answer so Friday evening he showed up at my door after his shift. I told him I had dinner plans with my sister downtown at Iron Cactus.

"Oh yeah, that's right. I forgot about that invite. Do you still want me to go with you?" he said.

"I don't care what you do, Tony."

But of course, he decided to tag along.

God answered my prayers in a matter of roughly one week. Teresa had called the previous week inviting us to dinner with her, her sister-in-law, Lawrence, Grant Alexander and a mutual female friend of Grant's and Teresa's. For whatever reason, the female friend was pretending to be Grant's wife; but I found out later that they were not even dating, but she was hanging around hoping to change his mind about their relationship. That was very hilarious to me. She had even bragged about how big and beautiful his new home was and pretended to be staying there alone and afraid while he was working overseas.

We all decided to car pool to the restaurant and Tony hopped in the back of Grant's Lexus, apparently, he did not want me to ride with him. So I rode in the car with Teresa, Lawrence and Christine, Lawrence's sister. I had known Grant since we were kids and had a huge crush on him, but I had not seen him in about a decade. He was still tall and very handsome with smooth chocolate skin and mucho swag on deck. He told me he had been asking Teresa about me over the years when he'd come home from the military to visit; but I was never around when he came to town. .

Teresa had organized the dinner outing because Grant was about to return to work in Afghanistan. He and I were laughing and talking as if neither of us had a date at the table. In hindsight, neither of us really did because I had already decided to break up with Tony and the girl that tagged along with him was not his date either. Grant asked me about my job working from home for Neiman Marcus and I text him the career site information. He said he had been working overseas for the last seven years and was ready to return home and work in the U.S.

The very next day, Grant asked Teresa to invite me over to his home with all of them for a game night. I had every intention of going by myself, but because Tony could tell he was skating on thin ice, he opted to show up again unannounced after work and go with me at the very last second when I was ready to pull out of my garage. We went over and there were a few more people there, but not the girl from the night before, so I asked Teresa where Grant's wife was and that's when she told me they were not a couple and certainly not married.

I sat down to watch Tony, Teresa, and some other people play spades because jokingly, no one wanted me on their team. Let's just say I can play the game, but I'm not the best partner to have. My feet are always cold and Teresa saw me shivering and suggested that I ask Grant for a blanket and some socks. He gladly invited me into his master suite to retrieve some socks and we were catching up a little as I stood at the door. Although I was done with Tony, I still didn't want to disrespect and embarrass him in anyway. I came back out with the socks and sat at the table again. Grant began jokingly motioning for me to come over by him and I laughed it off. I honestly did not know he was flirting with me until the next day.

Tony was not coming over that Sunday because he had a basketball game to watch with his dad. I received a text from Grant that morning saying, *Hey you! Please tell Kenya I'm sorry I didn't get to see her while I was home, hopefully next time she and her husband Chris can go to dinner with us as well.*

At first glance I knew, "hey you" was like what's up! But I wasn't sure, so I simply replied to his messages saying, *I'll let her know and that it was very good to see him. I wish we had more time to catch up, but maybe next time.* He asked if I was living in Cedar Hill and I told him yes and he text that he and his cousin Mitch were about to meet up at the Cedar Hill Walmart. I told him that was right around the corner from me and that I had not seen Mitch in over ten years and they should stop by if they had time. He asked me to text him my address and the directions and after I sent them to him, Tony called. I told him Grant and Mitch were about to stop by and he said that he was cool with it because he knew I had not seen either of them in forever and we had all grown up together.

Grant and Mitch arrived at my house in no time. When they pulled up out front, my children were looking out of the game room window and ran downstairs to notify me. The three of us sat in my den laughing, talking, watching television and catching up for about two hours. At the end of our visit, Grant asked me about my relationship with Tony and I told him it was pretty much over. He didn't even attempt to show any remorse; it was so funny. He was looking at some pictures of Tony and me on my mantle and joking by saying they needed to come down.

We were really vibing with one another, but I was still half mixed up in a situation and he was getting ready to leave and head back to Afghanistan in two days. When they left, Grant gave me a long, drawn out hug, and encouraged me to keep in touch with him. I agreed that I would keep in touch, but I was still a little uncertain about the extent of what he was insinuating, but very certain that either way, I could no longer drag out the doom of what were once The Nikki and Tony Show.

So the next day after plenty of encouraging words from Quita and Monique, I finalized my inevitable break up with Tony Daniels. He was very upset, but not at all violent. He begged, pleaded and refused to take no for an answer at first. I told him that I just didn't believe we should be together anymore and wasting both of our time. I invited him to come over on the weekend to pick up some items he had left at my house. He finally realized that he was not going to convince me to change my mind and agreed to cut ties. I felt like a huge weight had been lifted from my shoulders because I had prolonged the failed relationship in an effort to keep from hurting his feelings. But at the end of the day, I have no idea why I was worried about that, because he cared nothing about my feelings as shown in the text from Sammy Davis Jr. and several other inconspicuous indicators.

Grant was elated to hear that Tony and I had finally broken up. He then made it very clear that he wanted to keep in contact with me by phone, email, Skype, etc. I wasn't sure what that would lead to, but I enjoyed Grant's conversation and his hilarious personality. I was so intrigued by him and glad I didn't allow my recent experience with Tony to deter me from giving Grant an opportunity to get to know me all over again. Although I had known Grant since the '80s, we still did not really know one another because our lives had taken such very different paths over the last several years, so it was very exciting to become reacquainted with him again. He had also experienced a terrible marriage, had four sons, had traveled the world, and served in the military. He worked in Afghanistan as a fuel distributor under contract and took his R&R at home every two or three months.

We started out mostly emailing back and forth and then we began to talk about our expectations when in a relationship. In a very short time, we were spending six to eight hours every day talking on the phone; so much so that the bill ran up to a whopping $2,500! It's amazing how fast we jelled and developed feelings for one another being 7,714 miles apart for months on end.

One day he asked, "What's going on with us?"

"I'm not really sure yet, but whatever it is, it just feels so right and wonderful!"

"It really does feel very right. The reason I asked that question is because I'm glad it's turning out the way I actually thought it would because I can do anything as long as you got my back, Nikki."

"I got your back, as I told you before, when I'm with you, I'm with you."

"I'll definitely have yours too. If you need anything from me, baby...please just tell me!"

I've been through many storms, but being with Grant was starting to feel like my happiness was finally manifesting into something real. I couldn't help but be excited to see where the journey with him would lead me.

We had been dating for almost two years and the entire experience had been mind-blowing to say the least. He treated me like a queen and he sent me gift after gift to the front door literally every other day. It wasn't the gifts that made me love him so much, but it was his thoughtfulness and honesty that won me over. For him to think of me that way still makes my heart melt to this day. I've never had anyone express so much love for me.

When he would come home, we were inseparable. He would hang out with me at home for my entire eight-hour work shift, then go to school with me at night and wait for my classes to end. With us adding one another to our respective bank accounts early on in our relationship, and me keeping him informed of everything that went on with the kids and me on a daily basis, it felt like we were already married. We both have a mutual respect and undeniable love for each other. We had hit it off so well that it seemed like we had been together much longer than we had. Trust was a huge factor in building a solid foundation for our relationship, and we both participated in open and honest communication.

When Grant would come home on one of his R&R vacations, I was so excited to see him that I would run to him in the airport every time, almost knocking him down. On one particular time when he arrived, he asked me to buy a new outfit and to be prepared for a special date because he had made reservations for us. To my surprise, he took me out to a very romantic dinner and at the end of the night, he proposed to me. He had a beautiful, huge Robbins Brothers ring in the box with a light in it. I was completely thrilled. I had never pressured him because we had both been married before, so we were equally cautious of trying it again. But I was elated at saying yes to him and becoming his wife. I could not wait to call Grandmomma Emily to tell her. She absolutely loved Grant; she would always ask what I cooked for him when he was home.

The events leading up to our wedding were so exciting; stressful at times from lack of full participation from some of the wedding party, but still exciting. My best friend, Chanique, gave me a bridal shower in my home and she pulled out all the stops. She provided games, decorations, food, and a beautiful cake. Grandmomma Emily came to my bridal shower and was full of life, spunk, and laughter as always. Momma did not show up and everyone began asking me why, but who really knows. Chanique tearfully spoke at the end about all of the hard things in life she and I had faced together since becoming best friends in 1985. She has been there for me through good times and bad just like Monique.

Monique, and some other friends, planned my bachelorette party and they did not disappoint. I'll just leave it at that! Needless to say, it was a night to remember and we all had a blast. I was happy that Kenya and Teresa came also; it felt great to kick back and have fun with my sisters and my closest friends and family. My relationship with Kenya and Teresa is still not where I would like for it to be today, but it's much better than before. Maybe we need Iyanla Vanzant to come for a visit. God has even begun to heal my relationships with Momma, Grandmomma San, and my aunts. Daddy and I are cordial, but we still have some getting to know one another to do. However, I was happy that all of me and Grant's family came out to our wedding to support our union.

Our wedding was on May 4, 2013; the best day of my life! We had a huge and beautiful ceremony with two hundred and fifty guests and a wedding party of eighteen. Gospel recording artist Toryn Fowler sung her rendition of "The Lord's Prayer" and just blew us away with her beautiful voice. She also helped me get into both of my dresses for the evening.

The ceremony was catered and the layout was very elegant with cream lilies and linen table cloths. Momma helped our coordinator put the finishing touches on the decorations and that made me feel wonderful. Grandmomma Emily saw the huge portrait of me at the entrance of the venue in my pre-wedding dress and jokingly asked, "Who is that white lady you got hanging up at the front?" We laughed and I told her it was me, just with makeup and eyelashes!

Grant and I left the venue around midnight because he had booked us an elaborate honeymoon suite at the Grand Hyatt DFW. By the time we went home to pack for our honeymoon, we got to the hotel so late that we really didn't get a chance to enjoy all of its awesome amenities. Plus, we had an early flight to St. Lucia to the Sandals Grande St. Lucian Resort. The next morning, we arrived too late to check our bag and had to abruptly abandoned our larger suitcase. The airport staff offered us a huge, florescent blue trash bag for our clothing. This was hilarious to me because I was determined not to have to catch a later flight, but Grant is very easily embarrassed. He once nearly ran out of

Walmart when I pulled down a can of biscuits and all of them began to roll off the shelf. So carrying the florescent trash bag was like making him walk through the airport in his underwear. His priceless facial expressions made this experience all the more memorable. I was in stitches laughing.

We finally arrived in beautiful, picture perfect St. Lucia, but the ride from the airport was like an hour long because the resort was located on its own peninsula off the coast of the Atlantic Ocean. We spent a blissful seven days in our lovely suite in paradise. Our marriage was already off to a great start. Grant was so excited that he left his job in Afghanistan and decided to come home to be with me and the kids.

I call Grandmomma Emily at least once or twice a week to check on her and because I also love to hear her laugh and impart her wisdom. She is a very honest and outspoken individual, but she absolutely loves to laugh. She's very fond of Grant and is always sure to ask about him when I speak to her. He enjoys speaking to her too, even though she talks so fast he can only make out certain words so I have to translate for him on a regular basis. I have been around her my whole life, so I can pick up on what she says very well. One day when I spoke to her, she told me that she had been to the doctor because her back had been hurting so badly that she could not sleep and they may have found something on her MRI. I didn't think much of it because she would always down play things to keep us from worrying about her. Plus, she was seventy-six years young and still very independent and vibrant, so I was used to hearing about her frequent trips to the doctor. But that time was more different than I had realized. She had been previously diagnosed with breast cancer and given a year to live thirty-one years ago, so her testimony was already phenomenal.

The cancer had begun to attack her bones this time. It was spreading onto her hip, brain, spine, and two spots above her adrenaline glands. The one on her spine was causing the back pain she was experiencing, but the one in her hip had grown so large that it was threatening to fracture her hip bone. Once they found the cancer, Grandmomma Emily was in the hospital for about three weeks straight, taking test after test. They finally released her to go home, and she was determined to be around the entire family so Alvin Jr. had a family dinner at his house for her on May 25, 2014.

Grant and I came to the dinner after London's seventh birthday party at our home. Grandmomma Emily was feeling tired and getting into the car to leave as we arrived. I was glad I had a chance to see her before she left. Grant took pictures of me and her as she sat in the front seat of Uncle James' truck. I never really realized just how much I look like her until I looked at the pictures.

Grant and I went to her house later that week to take care of her. She was weak and she had been vomiting and complaining that her stomach was hurting. She asked me to call her doctor and we left a message with the nurse of her symptoms. Grandmomma Emily thought that maybe the medicine he'd prescribed for her was causing her stomach to be upset. She asked us to go to the store to get her some 7Up, and Grant and I walked to Little World; the corner store I'd frequented a thousand times as a child.

When we returned from the store, Grandmomma Emily drank a

very small amount of the 7Up and began to fall back to sleep. Grant sat in the room with her while I put her trash out and cleaned her rest-room. We stayed for a few hours and just sat there watching her sleep. As the afternoon came, I called Daddy to tell him that the nurse said she would have the doctor call him once he was available to talk about Grandmomma Emily. Grant had to get home and get ready for work, so I kissed her goodbye and she thanked us for coming by and then she went right back to sleep.

Aunt Shan, Uncle Curtis's wife, had been instrumental in help-ing take care of Grandmomma Emily and keeping me updated on her status. She was usually with her when I couldn't be there. When I spoke to her later on, she told me that Grandmomma Emily had gone to the doctor later that evening because the pain in her stomach was caused by an ulcer that had erupted and was leaking toxins from her small intestines into her stomach. The doctor ended up performing an emergency surgery on Grandmomma Emily and she was back in the hospital; but this time, she ended up in I.C.U. and stayed there for what felt like another month afterward.

It was hard to see her like that because she could not speak and she slept for days on end. We all would gather at the hospital to visit her frequently, even after she was transferred to a nice rehab facility near downtown Dallas. She ended up losing an astronomical amount of weight from not being able to eat solid foods for weeks on end. Her body was very weak and sore from being immobile for so long, but she was finally a little more vocal and starting to eat more.

One morning during my prayer time, I wrote Grandmomma Emily

a love letter while she was in I.C.U. I thought her health was finally turning around and that she would be home and back to her normal self in no time after a little physical therapy. I went to visit her at the rehab facility and she was sound asleep, so I sat quietly next to her bed and took a picture of her. When she opened her eyes and saw me there, she smiled and asked me for some lip chap. I gave her some of the lip gloss I kept in my purse and she went back to sleep.

The physical therapist and Aunt Shan arrived while I was sitting there and the therapist woke Grandmomma Emily up. He wanted her to move her legs and sit up on the edge of the bed, but she screamed in such agony that it was too much to bear. I helped him hold her legs up as tears fell from my eyes in sorrow for my dear sweet Grandmother. I had never seen her that way before. I asked Aunt Shan if the radiation for the cancer was helping and she informed me that the doctors had said her cancer was at Stage 4. I was so upset. I had to leave because I didn't want Grandmomma Emily to hear me weeping into Aunt Shan's shoulder as she hugged me.

I had to gather myself in the parking lot in order to drive home because I was so upset that I nearly drove my new truck down a one-way street. Just four days later, I awoke at 4:00 a.m. as I normally do, and I saw that I had about nine missed calls from Daddy, Aunt Shan, Bridgette, and Alvin Jr. I didn't know what to expect, but I called Alvin Jr. and Bridgette back and they told me to get to Baylor Hospital immediately. The urgency in their voices alarmed me. Grandmomma Emily was at the rehab facility and her heart had stopped in the middle of the night. She was unresponsive when she arrived at Baylor. They put her on life support and we spent hours watching her machine and

269

praying the numbers would go back up to indicate she was going to be okay.

Grandmomma Emily passed away before my dad and uncles could get the hospital staff to take her off of life support. Our entire family was in the room with her when she left. I was sitting at the foot of her bed with my hands on her legs, praying and it was like being in a *Lifetime* movie. The machine flat lined and began to beep and we all wept aloud. Momma and I had gotten so close that she brought Miracle to the hospital with her to be by my side. That meant the world to me. I had always wanted that type of rapport with my mother. I'm so thankful for God's healing.

Grandmomma Emily died on June 25, 2014; just four days before her seventy-seventh birthday. She was laid to rest with a beautiful ceremony at her church, Oak Hill Baptist Church, in South Dallas, on July 3, 2014. They had her long, pretty hair all dolled up and she had on makeup and lipstick. She was gorgeous! I sang "I Need You Now" by Smorkie Norful at her funeral. I closed my eyes and sung as if she was there listening because she had always loved to hear me sing. I had a moment when I almost lost it as I turned to her casket and sang those touching lyrics, but I kept it together.

Momma, Grandmomma San, my aunts, and my sisters attended the wake and funeral to support me. I was so happy to see them there because they have been coming around to support me more and God is still healing our relationships as well. Yolita, Hayden, his new wife, and several members from my old church were also in attendance. I am happy for Hayden and I pray for his new marriage, his well-being, and that we will continue to be friends and excellent co-parents.

Martha came to the funeral with Pastor Tatum, he was officiating. My relationship with Martha has gotten much better now that some years have passed since Hayden and I divorced, so I was very happy to see her there. Daddy still attends church with the Tatum family and I'm okay with that because he's been a member there for about seven years now and I can tell he's grown some under Pastor Tatum's ministry. I miss hearing Pastor Tatum's preaching, but I recently wrote him a letter telling him how much I still respect and love him as a father figure and thanked him for all he had taught me about the Bible.

Grandpa Howard sat on the front row at the funeral, but he has Alzheimer's now, so since the funeral, he forgot that Grandmomma Emily had passed away.. He called Alvin Jr. on the 4th of July and he had to be reminded again that we she was gone and that we had a funeral for her. With my Grandfather's health deteriorating and losing my Grandmother who meant so much to me, I began to revisit a brief low. The same kind of depression that after Hayden, I thought I would never experience again. I still catch myself thinking of her and reaching for the phone to call her. But God is my comforter and my strength and He'll never put more on me than I can handle. After surviving ten years of marriage to Hayden, I can certainly make it through anything else.

Now that I can laugh about such a dark time in my past with Hayden, I jokingly say that I was one decision away from having my own episode of "Snapped" on the *Oxygen* network. I can honestly identify with how someone can be pushed to their absolute breaking point and not be able to bear any more pain. So much so, that they re-sort to end it by any means necessary. But I never take for granted that thankfully, God did not allow my story to pan out with those results. It's interesting to see the expressions of people who have never expe-rienced depression when they hear my testimony. Some are compas-sionate and inspired; others are so religious that they can't help but to be judgmental and immediately question my salvation.

Even as a child, I used to wish I could just crawl into a small space and shut the rest of the world out. I imagined it as some form of pro-tection from the constant turmoil in my life. God has shown me over the years that He is my protection and the redeemer of all that was lost in my life. The only way I was able to be free from the debilitating restraints of the negative mindset that I had developed, was through forgiveness. It was truly a journey and an extensive growth process for me to arrive at this point. Only then was I able to exhale. Before I felt that, no one in my life had earned the right for me to express my vulnerability, so I carried a lot of pain inside of me for many years without speaking about it.

Since moving on with my life, I was told later on that A.B. had a stroke and now has Dementia and lives in a local nursing home. By the time I learned of his condition, my faith in God had grown tremen-dously and I wanted to go and visit him. I just wanted to let him know that I had forgiven him and that Christ loves him no matter what. What I have come to understand is that Christ died on the cross not only for my sins, but for his as well and his salvation to me is more important than any lifelong grudge that I could hold. The only person holding a grudge against him would hurt in the long run is me, through bitterness. Unfortunately, even though I tried, I was never able to retrieve A.B.'s contact information. But I believe that if I never see him again, God knows my heart has released him and that's all that matters.

I now realize that the way I dealt with the experiences of my childhood is parallel to the way that I dealt with the hurt I had experienced as an adult. However, in spite of not having positive examples of marriage and parenting in my life, God is allowing me to learn the right ways to parent, and by the grace of God, I am an awesome wife to Grant.

Writing this book gave me such a release and brought healing in so many areas of my life. The most enormous of them all was when God healed my mind and my heart from pornography. I've gone many years now without watching it, but the key is guarding my spirit to avoid the possibility of the temptation. I don't indulge in movies with excessive sex scenes. It was not until after I read *Battlefield of the Mind* by Joyce Meyer, that I learned how to be in control of my thoughts and to bring them into subjection with the Word.

When I began to pray and ask God to renew my mind in Christ and using His Word to fight the enemy, the more control I gained over all of the wrong thinking habits I had developed over the years. 2 Corinthians 10: 4-5 really helped me with this. It says, "The weapons we fight with are not the weapons of the world. On the contrary, they have divine power to demolish strongholds. We demolish arguments and every pretension that sets itself up against the knowledge of God, and we take captive every thought to make it obedient to Christ." In other words, don't allow just any thought to cross your mind and be entertained by it. Feed your spiritual man with the Word of God and not with anything that He would not approve of or that does not line up with His Word.

Renewing your mind in Christ is such a wonderful experience; it gives you inner peace and a continuous thirst for God's wisdom. Make a commitment to take this step. Remember that just because you've decided to get your thought life in check, does not mean Satan isn't going to continue to wage war against your mind. God has removed this sin and its desire from me completely. After hearing a sermon one Sunday, I received another aha moment and gained a new perspective to look at it as having sex with Satan himself. I knew I was saved and that Christ lives in me and I didn't want to continue to break His heart anymore

Other than my moments of procrastination, I think it took me so many years to finish writing this book because I was still healing and growing and God was not done allowing my story to come into fruition. You too can experience the peace and power of God in your heart. Ask Jesus to come into your heart and lean on Him to carry you through the good and bad times of this journey called life.

What I've learned from my collaboration of life lessons is that I am not my past or all of the ugly things that happened to me. I am the possibility of what can be and the voice of those who have also been molested, felt unwanted, that have been partakers of many sins and cast away, or who have had to suffer through domestic violence. The opinions that others formed about my life or me as a person, were predicated on numerous false assumptions, and I refuse to live up to what they postulate my life to be. I am who God says I am! I must be the best human being I can possibly be. Doing right may not reap expedient rewards or be profitable at all, but I believe it will bring peace to my soul to simply do the right things and treat others as I would like to be treated.

When I align with the center of myself where God abides, the flow of His purpose and His direction for my life is undeniable. Philippians 1:6 says, "For I am confident of this very thing, that He who has begun a good work in you will perfect it until the day of Christ Jesus." God did not lead me to write every personal detail of my life for exploitation nor to bring shame to the people I also wrote about. He led me to write this book for His edification; to show the world that if He can save and deliver someone as twisted up as I was, He can save anyone. I am humbled by His wanting my truth to be read by millions in an effort to bless the lives of hurting people all over the globe.

I am prepared for the next chapter of my life with Grant and the bright future of our awesome family. By faith, I am confident that something unimaginably wonderful is on the horizon for my life. I will forever believe that what the Devil meant for bad, God certainly used for my good.

THE END

About the Author

Nikki Alexander grew up in the inner city and graduated from Lincoln High School in the southern sector of Dallas. She has been in the telecommunications industry for fourteen years and is currently a Finance Specialist at one of the leading mobility companies in the United States. Her gruesome life experiences and triumphs in this tell-all autobiography will certainly define the trials and tribulations that she endured and overcame. Her source of motivation and encouragement to other survivors of mental, physical and emotional abuse is very transparent. She is enthusiastic about this book and the lives that it will touch. Nikki volunteers independently, as well as with business owners and nonprofit organizations, as a tangible means to provide for those in need. She still resides in Texas with her husband and four children – three daughters and one son. For more information about the author, she can be reached directly via email at: nikkialexauthor@gmail.com, or you may visit her online on at www.nikkialex.net.

www.ingramcontent.com/pod-product-compliance
Lightning Source LLC
Chambersburg PA
CBHW060008100426
42740CB00010B/1435